The 'Noble Gyn' of Comedy
in the Middle English Cycle Plays

American University Studies

Series IV
English Language and Literature
Vol. 79

PETER LANG
New York • Bern • Frankfurt am Main • Paris

Virginia Schaefer Carroll

The 'Noble Gyn' of Comedy in the Middle English Cycle Plays

PETER LANG
New York • Bern • Frankfurt am Main • Paris

Library of Congress Cataloging-in-Publication Data

Carroll, Virginia Schaefer
    The "Noble Gyn" of comedy in the Middle English
cycle plays.

    (American University studies. Series IV, English
language and literature ; vol. 79)
    Bibliography: p.
    Includes index.
    1. English drama — Middle English, 1100-1500 —
History and criticism. 2. Mysteries and miracle-plays,
English — History and criticism. 3. English drama
(Comedy) — History and criticism. 4. Christian drama,
English — History and criticism. 5. Bible in
literature. I. Title. II. Series.
PR643.M8C37   1989   822'.0516'0917   88-13077
ISBN 0-8204-0714-3
ISSN 0741-0700

CIP-Titelaufnahme der Deutschen Bibliothek

Carroll, Virginia Schaefer:
The "noble gyn" of comedy in the middle
English cycle plays / Virginia Schaefer Carroll.
— New York; Bern; Frankfurt am Main; Paris:
Lang, 1989.
    (American University Studies: Ser. 4,
    English Language and Literature; Vol. 79)
    ISBN 0-8204-0714-3

NE: American University Studies / 04

© Peter Lang Publishing, Inc., New York 1989

All rights reserved.
Reprint or reproduction, even partially, in all forms such as microfilm,
xerography, microfiche, microcard, offset strictly prohibited.

Printed by Weihert-Druck GmbH, Darmstadt, West Germany

for Allan

TABLE OF CONTENTS

CHAPTER 1: Comedy in the Cycle Plays 1

    The "Problem" of Comedy in the Cycle Plays. 1

    The "Noble Gyn" of Comedy 17

CHAPTER 2: Old Testament Challenges to Authority 31

    Creation. 32

    Cain and Abel 40

    Noah and His Wife 66

    Summary 96

CHAPTER 3: Comic Questioning of the Incarnation. 107

    Joseph's Trouble about Mary 108

    The Shepherds and Other Doubters. 130

CHAPTER 4: Tense Comedy in the New Testament Plays . . .171

    Massacre of the Innocents 172

    The Passion Plays 183

CONCLUSION 215

BIBLIOGRAPHY 223

INDEX. 239

CHAPTER 1:
Comedy in the Cycle Plays

The fact that comedy exists in the Middle English cycle plays is indisputable: one need look only as far as the plays depicting the fall of Lucifer to see an unusual comic effect at work. A more important issue, then, is the purpose of this comedy. The distinctiveness of this humor lies in its ability to take strength and substance from the deeply religious context in which it is placed. Although juxtaposition of earthly to religious perspectives is characteristic of the art and literature of the Middle Ages, the cycle playwrights use this apparent contrast as a source of both dramatic tension and thematic resolution.

This chapter seeks to place this distinctive fact about medieval drama in a proper critical framework by first considering critical perspectives of comedy within the cycles.

The "Problem" of Comedy in the Cycle Plays

Because many early critics ignored the comic elements of the cycles--choosing instead to focus their attention on the simple, primitive piety in the Age of Faith that was the Middle Ages--and because nineteenth-century criticism encouraged the application of Darwinian evolution even to a study of English drama, the cycle plays were praised for decades solely in terms of their existence as examples of popular devotion and as the crude, but fertile, soil from which Renaissance drama sprang.

2

The titles alone of early critical editions of Middle English drama betray their editors' propensity for paradoxical views of these plays: they find in the cycle plays many of the essential characteristics of English drama, yet they pointedly scoff at what they consider its embryonic stage. In 1897, J.M. Manly published Specimens of the Pre-Shakespearean Drama, a work which is appropriately titled, for it glances at the plays only backwards, over Shakespeare's shoulder, and shudders at what it sees.[1] Similar in title and attitude is Chief Pre-Shakespearean Dramas by J.Q. Adams.[2] Strangely, although these editors find some of the Middle English plays interesting enough to anthologize, they simply cannot accept the manuscripts as intentional artistic achievement; therefore, they include only bowdlerized versions of any plays that might be offensive, editing extensively what are now considered some of the highest achievements of medieval drama.

These examples are extreme, but a similar underlying attitude--if not actual critical development--pervades many of the subsequent studies of Middle English cycle drama. As O.B. Hardison suggests, the scientific developments of the last century, both Darwin's contribution and the refinement of the scientific method, led scholars to attempt to authenticate their studies by placing under microscope and in Petri dish the literary organisms they wished to observe.[3] The English drama was an ideal subject for this type of examination, Hardison explains, because, with some selective consideration of available data, it appears to show continuous development in isolation. Also, such an hypothesis made respectable the previously held assumptions regarding the dramatic organism and the literary periods of England: drama germinates in simple medieval beginnings; flowers in Marlowe, Shakespeare, and Jonson; and ages and withers until its death in 1642. A clear example of this approach is The Mediaeval Stage by E.K. Chambers.[4] Although it is still unsurpassed as a compendium of medieval records and sources regarding the plays, the reader almost always senses the writer's conscientiousness in covering his theoretical frame with a starched, white laboratory coat.

Much less subtle is W.W. Greg's study of the plays, for he openly uses terms associated with biological and evolutionary development to describe the transformation from liturgical to secular drama. He speaks of "spontaneous growth," "evolution of the drama," "embryonic stage," and the "chain of evolution" as he analyzes the secularization of biblical drama.[5] Albert C. Baugh, writing as late as 1948, uses the ideas of evolution as the source of both his vocabulary and his understanding of the drama. He refers to the tenth-century liturgical trope of the Easter service as ". . . the germ out of which modern drama grew."[6] One difficulty of this approach is that it attempts to fill in with conjecture the gaps that historical and textual records have left empty. The result is that the evolution theory seems solid, but is actually hollow, as this excerpt demonstrates:

> . . . additional episodes tended to develop, if not actually in the office, at least in a transitional stage ending in separation from the church. The birth of Christ, for example, called

> for some explanation. If Adam and Eve had not
> fallen, man would not have been in need of re-
> demption. A scene was needed showing the tempta-
> tion of Eve by Satan in the Garden of Eden. But
> why did Satan tempt Eve? Out of malice for
> having been driven out of heaven. Why was he
> driven out of heaven? That also must be told.
> Finally, the evil brought to the world by man's
> disobedience can be symbolized by the slaying of
> Abel by Cain.[7]

This theory of the thematic development of the cycles--and their
ultimate movement down the nave and out into the market-place--
was accepted for years. Critics looked to the liturgical drama
of medieval England as the source for the Corpus Christi plays,
and, in so doing, arrived at startling conclusions, especially
about the appearance and function of comedy in the plays.

Frederik Wood's assumptions about the medieval audience and
its need for humor led to a conclusion about the secularization
of the plays:

> Immediately the miracle plays, freed from cleri-
> cal control, fell into the hands of the towns-
> folk, familiar and realistic touches were added
> which brought them into close contact with medie-
> val life. The former austerity gradually disap-
> peared and a note of humanism was introduced.
> The themes were still essentially serious, but
> usually the serious side was left undeveloped,
> and the governing spirit became comic.[8]

The problem with this view is that, first of all, it attributes
the development of comedy to the inevitable, spontaneous growth
of the secular drama, instead of as a conscious artistic aim of
the playwrights. Wood's approach--like others which assume
dramatic evolution--also is misleading in that it puts serious
and comic elements in contention with one another for control of
the plays.[9] Such a distinction establishes a polarity between

seeming opposites which is not, in fact, present in all of the plays; and it suggests that the religious feeling and intention of the mystery plays became somehow corrupted and degraded in the hands of a primitive mob.

Fortunately, George R. Coffman's essay urged critics to examine the English mysteries with the careful scrutiny of a scientist but without the presumptions that had previously accompanied such an approach. Coffman defends the plays and suggests what, more than half a century later, seems obvious:

> . . . the four complete cycles, with fragments of others, and records of various kinds preserved furnish an adequate body of materials for interesting, comprehensive, and challenging studies.[10]

Coffman praises the critics who find the plays to be worthy of serious consideration, and catalogues the areas of important study: the liturgical and vernacular sources, the central themes in the cycles, the nature of revisions, the possible identities of the playwrights and redactors, and the textual suggestions for localities of the cycles. Yet Coffman asks more of those who study the Corpus Christi plays; he urges scholars to study "the dramatic effectiveness of the material selected."[11] As a result of Coffman's article and of increased interest in the plays themselves, studies of the Corpus Christi cycles took on new perspectives, especially with regard to analyses of those plays which had, for years, been respected.

A roughly chronological glance at criticism of the Secunda Pastorum reveals increasing awareness of the dramatic strengths of the play and provides an easily discernible pattern of critical attitudes toward the Corpus Christi drama as a whole. Gayley and Hemingway[12] are representative of the "old school," which was unable to reconcile the idea of comedy in a religious play. These critics praise the homespun comedy and rustic realism of the Secunda Pastorum, but they are skeptical about its integration into a religious cycle. Similarly ambiguous appreciation is evident in Baugh's treatment of the play. Although he praises it as an example of "'good theater' with boisterous humor and exuberance of spirit,"[13] he regards the Mak episode as an interesting folk-tale, not as a parallel to and important development of the Nativity theme:

> There is humor of situation and humor of dialogue and incidental allusion--jibes at shrewish wives and crying children, taxes and the poor man's lot. The length of the Mak episode is hopelessly out of proportion to the proper matter of the play. The Second Shepherds' Play as a shepherds' play is an artistic absurdity; as a farce of Mak the sheep-stealer it is the masterpiece of the English religious drama.[14]

He analyzes the nature of the humor in the play, but he overlooks its dramatic and religious function.

The publication of Homer Watt's essay on the unity of the play marked an important development in the consideration of the Secunda Pastorum, for it suggested that the traditional view of unity--unity of plot--is superseded in this play by a unity of theme.[15] Watt counters two of the usual criteria that make the play appear disunified: the fact that the biblical narrative comprises less than one-fifth of the drama, and the portrayal of the main characters as English, not Palestinian, shepherds. His study, therefore, allows the Wakefield Master these apparent incongruities and chooses as its focus the dramatic development of the childbirth theme. Francis Thompson also gives credit to the playwright as he assesses the levels of meaning implied in such an unusual juxtaposition of comic and religious themes. Most revealing is his statement that one need not exclude one level of meaning in order to understand another:

> The artist who wrote the play most certainly was familiar with the medieval theory that a given text might have several senses at one and the same time.[16]

His development of this theory in its application to the Mak episode is disappointing, however, for Thompson mechanically outlines the literal, allegorical, moral, and anagogical levels in the play without ever suggesting a theory for the ways that these levels work together.

Robert Cosbey's study of the analogues of the Mak story, while not specifically addressing the question of the purpose of comedy, seeks to present a previously unstated declaration of the skill of the Wakefield Master. Cosbey compares eleven similar versions of the story of Mak and theorizes about the possible explanations for such striking resemblances among tales that span five centuries and six nations. What results from his investigation is that Cosbey limns not only the valuable source material that folklore provided for the medieval English playwrights, but also the considerable amount of skill and care used in honing this material and adapting it to the dramatic purpose of the play:

> We can conclude fairly safely then, it seems, that the Wakefield playwright did make use of a folk-tale. . . . The differences between the Mak

version and the others are important, for they show what the Wakefield playwright added to his source, and how he shaped it to fit his dramatic needs.[17]

Such an understanding marks two important steps in criticism of the cycle plays, as well as of the methods of the Wakefield Master. First, it assumes that the writers of the plays were able dramatists, whose deviations from the biblical and traditional narratives should be viewed as conscious, artistic intention--not error or the uncontrollable urge to secularize the religious plays. Secondly, Cosbey's study supplies an important focus for critics of the mysteries: to understand how and why the playwrights chose to develop their subject matter.

Several recent studies investigate the Secunda Pastorum with the specific perspective that Cosbey suggests. Applying E. Catherine Dunn's discussion of the Towneley cycle Old Testament plays[18] to the Nativity play of that cycle, William M. Manly states that the prophetic principle--not only the structural parallels between the religious story and its parody--serves to unify the play. While not denying the comic episodes, Manly views the play as "felt religious drama,"[19] for he sees "insistent and continuing emphasis on Christ and Christianity in the emotional language of the shepherds who are awaiting Christ's birth."[20] More importantly, Manly attempts to reconcile the religious and dramatic implications of the opening remarks of the shepherds:

> The oaths and exclamations of the shepherds are not grasped intellectually or theologically but are used instinctively. An important effect of this instinctive piety is to place emphasis on traditional religious responses and to incorpo-

rate into the immediate, temporal moment of the
Nativity a sense of ritual re-presentation. The
Towneley playwright, by using anachronisms of
this sort, has allowed his shepherds to function
unconsciously as a Process prophetarum and has
thus reinforced that sense of atemporal or non-
sequential unity which is generated by the cy-
clical presentation of the mystery plays as a
whole.[21]

Such a statement suggests not only a very talented dramatist,
but also a deliberate emotional and theological complexity in
the presentation of the Nativity scene. Manly, always keeping
sight of the religious intention of the play, further investi-
gates its antithetical nature by examining the backdrop of the
Antichrist legend that he views as important for the Mak episode. In a related study, Linda E. Marshall focuses on and
develops the function of this Antichrist legend in the play.
She traces the growth of the legend in medieval secular and
religious literature and concludes with this explanation for its
presence in the Secunda Pastorum:

. . . the Antitypes of Christ serve to elucidate
both doctrine and artistic design more clearly,
since their perverted copies of goodness can only
help to retrace their source.[22]

The most recent critical studies focus on this aspect of
the play, asking in what way a drama with such complex and
secular tangents is able to lead its audience meaningfully to
the concluding revelation in the stable. Maynard Mack, Jr.,
suggests that the Mak episode functions thematically to remind
the audience of the mysteries implied in the Nativity.[23] The
drama occurs as much in the minds of the members of the audience
as it does on the stage before them, Mack asserts, and it is the

resulting realization of the audience's religious expectations that becomes the moving force in the drama:

> Mak's dream of birth is thus transformed into _this_ birth; his magical incantation upon the sleeping shepherds into _this_ miracle; his disguising cloak into the mystery of the Word disguised in flesh; and the whole illogical farce structure, which drove the shepherds to Mak's house despite all his spells and plans, into a foretaste of the mysterious ways by which Providence moves (in the world as on stage), its wonders to perform.[24]

Mack thus views the play as exciting and vivid drama which leads its audience to a profound rediscovery of the mysteries of their faith. Rose A. Zimbardo adopts a similar view in her discussion of the comic mockery of the sacred, for she, too, sees that parody functions religiously as well as dramatically in the play.[25] Through parody, she suggests, the audience comes to understand its own limited perception of the sacred.

Josie Campbell, concentrating on the social function of farce in drama, discusses the role of the comedy in the _Prima Pastorum_ and _Secunda Pastorum_.[26] She asserts that comic action accentuates a dialectic present in the members of the audience and thereby elicits feeling and change from them. In the shepherds' plays, the viewers become more aware of, and even anxious about, the internal conflicts between their minds and bodies; therefore, they await with eagerness the "hinge" that the farce provides. And, Campbell points out, the farce comes to represent the mystery, not merely parallel it:

> The farce is shown to reveal the same interior truth that the Advent contains. In the shepherds' plays, farce itself is radical action that reveals the birth of something new, the positive act of the spirit of love, being generated para-

doxically from the implicit physical and material
decay inevitably present in all bodily gratification.   Thus, farce in these plays presents us
with a paradigm of even more radical action
contained within the mystery of the Incarnation,
where God becomes man according to the flesh, but
remains God according to the spirit.[27]

That comic action could actually serve to reinforce the reli-

gious themes implied in the Corpus Christi drama is therefore a

possibility that critics of these plays have come to accept.

This brief overview of critical treatment of the Secunda

Pastorum reveals that there has been a growing tendency to

credit the Wakefield Master with an ability to manipulate source

material--through vivid dialogue and lively staging--and reveal

his artistic and dramatic intentions. A question that still

arises, however, and one which this study seeks to address, is

whether one may generalize about the use of comedy in the mys-

tery cycles and explain specifically how the playwrights used

this vehicle to achieve their religious ends.

Critics have come to realize that many of the medieval

English cycle plays have at their core the dramatic tension

created by the juxtaposition of religious and comic elements.

Although some studies, such as those by Fry and Wood,[28] insist

that the humorous elements are not integral parts of the play

and that the religious aspects of the drama are completely

divorced from the sometimes comic developments, investigations

of the comic spirit in general suggest that there is a subtle,

inextricable bond between the lighthearted and the profoundly

serious.   In his examination of the features of early English

humor, for example, Louis Cazamian asserts that "humour essentially consists in a duality of meaning; and the serious reflective disposition of the English character. . . laid so to say a background of serious pensiveness behind the more external and superficial mood of everyday."[29]   Beatrice White explains that much of the merriment associated with medieval England can be linked to a yoking of apparent extremes that she finds unique to this age:

> Unlike the sophisticated, reasoned laugh, this laughter was spontaneous and primitive, freely provoked by the shock of unexpected contrasts or of opposed moods, encountered so frequently by the lettered and rich devout in the marginal illuminations to their Psalters, Breviaries, and Books of Hours, where malicious little creatures, grotesque and ridiculous, romped and frolicked unconcernedly round a solemn text which accentuated the absurdity of their pranks. [30]

This view of comedy may appropriately be applied to the mystery cycles, for there one discovers similar surprising contrasts between the traditional religious narrative and the funny—even coarsely funny—antics of the characters on stage.   Although there are suggestions that audiences viewed the humorous episodes in the context of Christian comedy, the rise from sorrow to joy,[31] it is important to remember that several of the plays are consciously designed to evoke the kind of spontaneous laughter that White describes.

V.A. Kolve, in his examination of the nature of religious humor, supports such a view.   While praising the medieval playwrights for their artistic control of humor in the cycle plays, Kolve asserts that one must not mistake control for an intention to evoke only smirks and muffled chortles.   Instead, Corpus

Christi drama

> often sought the vulgar guffaw, the laugh from
> the belly rather than the smile. And on occasion
> it valued this kind of laughter as an indication
> of sanity, indeed almost of holiness.[32]

Such laughter serves as an important feature of the world of play and game established by the cycle plays. As Kolve points out, even the etymology of the medieval term for vernacular drama links the sense of dramatic play with revelry. Instead of using those terms which describe liturgical drama--_ordo_ or _representatio_, for example--the mystery plays employed a rarer and more ambiguous term, _ludus_. Whether the primary meaning is amusement or a dramatic form remains unclear, but for Kolve, "this very ambiguity may prove an entrance into the medieval idea of theater, for it is this word _ludus_, in its English equivalents 'play' and 'game', that becomes the ubiquitous generic term for the vernacular drama."[33]

As several critics have suggested, the medieval dramatists' view of the cycle plays as games imposes a very different aesthetic from the modern theater of illusion. The audience remains conscious of itself and of the fact that the actors are only playing their parts. In the context of religious drama, such an aesthetic is both dramatically and theologically useful, for the dramatist is able to avoid blasphemy and to present large actions simply and swiftly.[34] The result, Kolve suggests, is that the cycle drama was understood as "a lie designed to tell the truth about reality."[35] Martin Stevens argues a similar point: "it is precisely the world of play through which the average spectator of the medieval Corpus Christi cycle came to confront the eternals of the Christian faith."[36]

Although Kolve and Stevens compare the theatrical experience offered by the cycle plays to the anti-illusionist theater of Bertolt Brecht, Merle Fifield and Claude Gauvin reject the analogy primarily on the basis of audience response. For example, Fifield argues that the emotive response to the cycle plays is directly opposed to the rational response sought by Brecht, who "abominated empathy and sympathy, catharsis. He hoped for a casual, cigar-smoking spectator."[37] Gauvin, too, argues for an emotional response, for he states that the aim of the plays was to construct "une immense 'image devotionelle', animée et parlante du schema de la Redemption."[38]

A clear paradox is suggested in these discussions of the theatrical aesthetic of the plays. Although the spectators are often reminded of the fact that they are witnessing illusion, they are nevertheless drawn into the game and respond emotionally to dramatized events. The players thus include not only the actors on stage, but also the members of the audience, who must submit themselves to the rules of the game. Traditional accusations of sacrilege and blasphemy are out of bounds, as are clear distinctions between seriousness and comedy, entertainment and education. The stance demanded by comedy is effective in achieving this level of participation, for the spectators simultaneously detach themselves intellectually and involve themselves freely and emotionally with the stage action.

The purpose of laughter is another important issue. An

essential distinction one must make regarding the humor in the mysteries is between the comedy which functions as a release from the devotional intensity of the religious theme and the comedy which functions dramatically, as a part of the intensity, to heighten audience awareness of the religious theme. Gayley argues that a religious intent necessarily characterizes the comedy as the kind of relief which is essential if the audience were to give close attention to the most important aspects of the cycles:

> . . . though the dramatic edifice constructed by our medieval forbears is generally comedy, it is also divine. And not for a moment did these builders lose their reverence for the House spiritual that was sacred, nor once forget that the stones which they ignorantly and often mirthfully swung into strange juxtaposition were themselves hewn by Other Hands. The comic scenes of the English Miracle should, therefore, be regarded not as interruptions to the sacred drama, nor as independent episodes, but as counterpoint or dramatic relief.[39]

For Gayley, this is the only possible reason for comedy to exist in the plays, and one senses in his attitude a spirit of awe and gratitude that some "Other Hands" molded what was best for the unlearned multitudes at the market-place. Clifford Davidson examines the function of the comic and realistic elements from a more useful perspective. He concludes his study of the York Passion Play by stating that "the conscious purpose of the York plays was . . . not to provide psychological release into dramatic game or entertainment. . . ."[40] Rather, the playwright strove, Davidson suggests, to use these elements to involve the audience and thereby "impress feelingly upon the people the spectacle of the Christian story."[41]

All of the plays are not successful in using comedy so effectively, and certainly a brief perusal of the texts of the four complete cycles--Chester, York, Towneley, and N-Town-- reveals that many of the plays lack the dynamism and attention to detail that are so often praised as characteristic of dramatists like the Wakefield Master and the York Realist. In these less skillfully drawn plays, one may concur with Gayley that the comic interludes seem only to serve as a kind of dramatic release, but this release itself is often a virtue, as Kolve notes: "the Middle Ages frequently used images of breaking or bursting to express [the] need for relaxation into laughter."[42] In the best plays, however, the comic action and characterization function intensely and dramatically to induce the members of the audience to grapple with the obscure elements of their faith. If they do not do so, then the plays fail on a theological--if not artistic--level, as Margery Morgan explains:

> If their laughter at the farce did not prepare the onlookers to be more deeply affected by the sacred climax, the dramatist had failed in his task despite all his ingenuity. [43]

Many of the plays are successful, however, precisely because the playwrights understand both the fine boundary between the ludicrous and the divine and the dramatic intensity necessary to transcend it. In the best plays of the Corpus Christi cycles, the writers use comedy as an effective spiritual device, leading the audience from the high-spirited to the highly spiritual.

The "Noble Gyn" of Comedy

A useful metaphor for the kinds of comedy one finds in the cycles is suggested in the Wakefield _Processus Noe_. In that play, both God and Noah refer to the ark as a "noble gyn," a magnificent, ingenious structure. This term is equally suitable as a terse description of the carefully designed comic structure of the plays.

The OED defines _gyn_ not only as "an instance or product of ingenuity" but also, in a more pejorative sense, as a "contrivance, scheme, device . . . cunning stratagem, artifice, trick." Both senses of the word are appropriate in a consideration of comedy in the plays. As shown in the brief discussion of the _Secunda Pastorum_, the cycle dramatists demonstrated considerable skill in weaving comic themes and characters through religious narratives. But the playwrights often used comedy for a greater purpose than making the spectators laugh: they imposed a useful and attractive artifice on the biblical narratives in order to bring the audience, unawares, to a state of greater spiritual understanding and acceptance. Even the specialized meaning of _gyn_ as "a contrivance for catching game" is useful here, for the spectators are lured, through their emotional involvement with the comic action, to participate in often vigorous struggles with their faith.

In addition to its capacity for tricking spectators, comedy in the cycle plays is sometimes characterized by its ennobling effect. Because the playwrights carefully control the comic episodes and characters, they are able to shift the intense comic involvement their plays inspire to strong involvement on a spiritual level. As a result, the comedy of the cycle plays is capable of bringing each spectator to a more personal resolution of religious doubts.

In several important aspects, the use of comedy to achieve such an effect reveals the cycle playwrights' sensitivity to the relation between religious and comic responses. One cannot explain, in terms that make sense to anyone else, why a certain joke is particularly amusing and why another joke barely elicits a smile. Because laughter--the most obvious but certainly not the only basis for measuring comic response--evolves from the complex, unique meshing of one's experiences and responses to them, each person's reaction to comedy is highly personal and, to a great extent, inexplicable. The abstract "sense of humor" is thus similar to the "sense of faith" an individual has, in that devotional responses to the same religious message or image vary widely among individuals and cannot be explained in logical terms. Although a person may offer homiletic analyses of the rational basis of his faith, the ultimate acceptance of that faith is the result of a personal, emotional choice which defies explanation. One may intellectualize a joke or an aspect of one's faith, but such explanations are distinct from the force of the response; quite simply, one laughs just as one believes, in spite of rational arguments which justify or discourage that response.

In the mystery cycles, the response invited by comedy is more than an analogy of the religious response that the plays inspire; it becomes the vehicle through which the spectators prepare themselves emotionally for the intense presentation of religious mysteries. Through the dynamic interplay of comic and profound elements in the plays, the dramatists suggest that the seat of faith in a person is situated quite close to the seat of humor. By eliciting response from one area, the playwright may be able to bridge the uncertain cleft between comedy and faith. In the plays, the deliberate exaggeration of comic detail charges the drama with intensity and encourages playful participation in the stage action; this intensity is transformed into profound devotion in the most successful plays, for the high plateau of emotion is sustained even as the subject matter shifts from coarse comedy to traditional biblical narrative. The result is not only a new way of looking at the familiar stories, but also--more importantly in the late Middle Ages--a new way of _feeling_ about one's faith.

The plays which present the incident of the woman taken in adultery, for example, expand the biblical narrative considerably to include raucously comic situations. As sources of lively dramatic counterpoint to the stasis of Christ's preaching, these seemingly inappropriate developments infuse life and energy into an otherwise colorless sermon on Christian forgiveness. On a religious level, however, these scenes evoke more than dramatic interest; they encourage the spectators, through their laughter at the scheming Pharisees and their victims, to feel security and joy in Christ's promise of mercy. The highly doctrinal point of the play is thus made appealing and involving through low comedy.

Although the other cycles briefly expand the biblical narrative, the N-Town play offers the most explicit development of comic suggestions. In a tightly constructed play which begins and ends with Christ's sermons on mercy, the N-Town dramatist contrasts the serious explanation of divine forgiveness with the games of the scribe, Pharisee, and accusator. The opening address, which outlines important features of true repentance, provides an impetus for both stage action and thematic development.

Upon hearing Christ's proclamation that "Who so Aske mercy he xal haue grace," the scribe laments that "oure Lawe is lorn"[44] and incites the others to ponder the action that they should take. Because they see Christ's principle of mercy as a serious threat to a law that is based on earthly systems of justice, the scribe, Pharisee, and accusator scheme to devise "a Ffals qwarel" (57) with which they can test and trap Christ. Although the biblical reference to their plot is brief and without comic suggestion,[45] the N-Town playwright invents a "ryght good sporte" (66) for them. It is not enough in this play to present an accused adulteress; instead, the proof of her sin is included in elaborate detail. The accusator's language in describing the suspected woman is tinged with more amusement than horror at her sin:

> A fayre ȝonge qwene here-by doth dwelle
> both ffresch and gay upon to loke
> And a tall man with here doth melle
> the wey in to hyre chawmere ryght evyn he toke.
>
> (69-72)

As soon as such an explicitly sexual situation is included, the play has potential for comic development, for, even within the serious context of Christ's ministry, the joke of surprising the lovers is appealing and humorous. The tone of the three men indicates this abrupt departure from the serious sermon which opens the play: with unrestrained delight in their play, they scurry toward the home of the adulteress, and their excitement encourages the spectators to anticipate the comic confrontation that they sense is coming.

When they break down the door which had previously secluded the lovers, the scene erupts in lively, bold comedy. The stage directions following line 124, for example, emphasize the humor --not the sin--of the situation:

> hic juuenis quidam extra currit indeploydo
> calligis non ligatis et braccas in manu tenens

The mere presence of this man--caught, literally, with his pants down--is comic in itself, but his anger and indignation under such circumstances develops the visual joke. He threatens to " eve a dedly wownde" (128) to anyone who tries to stone him, and he boldly claims, "I xal þis daggare putt in his croppe" (131). He speaks brave words, but his state of undress humorously emphasizes his vulnerability and his weakness.

Even after the young man runs away, cursing all of them "to þe devyl of helle" (136) and trying to tie his breeches, the scene continues on a comic level. The scribe and the Pharisee playfully accuse the woman, feigning shock and disgust at her adultery:

22

                                                    Scriba
Come forth þou stotte com forth þou scowte
com forth þou bysmare and brothel bolde
com forth þou hore and stynkynge bych clowte
how longe hast þou such harlotry holde.

                                                Phariseus
Com forth þou quene come forth þou scolde
com forth þou sloveyn com forth þou slutte
we xal the tecche with carys colde
A lytyl bettyr to kepe þi kutte.

                                        (145-52)

This taunting list of insults and obscenities reveals the relish
with which the scribe and Pharisee carry out their game. They
become so immersed in playing the role of righteous authorities
that they seem to forget temporarily that the woman is only bait
for a more important "catch."

From her first plea to those who accuse her, the adulteress
focuses the play once again on the theme of mercy and repentance. She begs, "Ffor goddys loue haue mercy on me" (154), a
skillfully worded request that has both dramatic and thematic
implications. The despair with which she invokes "goddys loue"
emphasizes both her awareness of being trapped and her willingness to beg pathetically to be spared. Although the prospect of
being stoned is not humorous, the presentation of such despair
is comic under these circumstances, since the Pharisee and
scribe are only playing a game. On a thematic level, her reminder of the importance of forgiveness for the sake of God's
love echoes an essential feature of Christ's opening sermon:
"Eche man to othyr be mercyable / And mercy he xal haue at nede"
(33-34).

In the dialogue that follows, the playwright keeps that

shadow of Christ's doctrine just below the surface of the lively exchange. Earthly systems of punishment and exoneration become caricatures of justice, especially since the accusers--and the adulteress herself--reveal their misunderstanding of Christian repentance. Because her outright plea for mercy fails, for example, the woman resorts to bribery and flattery to save herself from shame:

> Serys my wurchepp if ȝe wyl saue
> And helpe I haue non opyn shame
> bothe gold and sylvyr ȝe xul haue
> So þat in clennes ȝe kepe my name.
> (161-64)

Even more enjoyable than this brazen offer of money is the scribe's affected shock that she would even consider bribing men of such high principle. With tongue in cheek, the scribe is horrified at her offer and threatens to bring her to "a game" which will make a lesson of her. The conditional nature of earthly pardon is thus mocked by the playwright, and the false superiority of the scribe directly contradicts Christ's teaching that "evyn as þou woldyst he xulde þe" (30).

The woman's next request is an even more audacious twisting of the true meaning of repentance. Since she realizes that neither money nor sympathy can sway the men from their decision to stone her, the adulteress seeks not to repent in her heart, but to prevent public humiliation. She is concerned only about the shame that she and her friends will suffer if the accusers insist on public punishment: "I pray ȝow kylle me prevyly / lete not þe pepyl know my defame" (175-76). The most important condition for repentance--that the sinner acknowledge in her heart the seriousness of her sin and accept the penance which will free her of guilt--is blatantly overlooked here, as the dramatist plays with the idea that, according to earthly systems of atonement, having concealed the fact of one's crime is as good as having never committed it.

The playwright is careful to sustain dramatic interest as he subtly imposes such thematic contrasts, for the reactions of the accusers is openly comic. As if they were offended by her boldness and could think of no suitable punishment themselves, the accusers suggest that this "devyl of helle" (179) be brought before Christ for judgment. As they lead her to Christ--the action toward which the entire play has been building--they continue their raucous enjoyment of the game. They delight in pushing and slapping the adulteress, partly because they are only playing that they are morally superior and partly because, in their minds, the trap for Christ has been set so well.

The encounter with Christ brings an end to their merriment, however, for the accusers become caught in their own trap. In an enjoyable scene in which the villains are soundly defeated at their own game, the dramatist achieves satisfying dramatic and thematic resolution.

The conversion of the adulteress, for example, illustrates the genuine change of heart needed to believe in and accept God's mercy. Her first appeal to Christ is thus not only the dramatic turning point--a means of slowing the pace and focusing attention on Christ as he silently writes in the earth--but also the essential link between the comic scenes and the central theme of repentance:

> Now holy prophete be mercyable
> vpon me wrecch take no vengeaunce
> Ffor my synnys Abhomynable
> In hert I haue grett repentaunce
> I am wel wurthy to haue myschaunce
> Both bodyly deth and werdly shame
> but gracyous prophete of socurraunce
> þis tyme pray ȝow for goddys name.
>
> (209-16)

Although this passage echoes her earlier cry for mercy, the changed attitude of the adulteress reveals a more serious intention than trying to avoid humiliation. She confesses well in this speech, for she acknowledges both her own unworthiness and her strong faith and hope in God's forgiveness.

Most importantly, her confession gives her new strength and new direction in life. She vows, "I wyl nevyr more be so vnstable" (261) and promises "all my lewde lyff I xal doun lete / and ffonde to be goddys trewe servaunt" (283-84). Unlike her accusers, who are too enveloped in their own shame to seek mercy, the adulteress' faith ultimately outweighs her shame, and she gratefully accepts the consolation and absolution offered by Christ.

Because the spectators have witnessed the amusing presentation of human pardon in the earlier scenes of the play, they sustain high emotional involvement in its serious conclusion. Laughter at the accusers' jests thus becomes awe at the boundless mercy of God, and enjoyment of bawdy comedy turns to celebration on a religious--but no less emotional--level. As in the plays which focus on Creation, on the Nativity, and on Christ's Passion, this play succeeds in using comedy as a "noble gyn," capable of involving the audience intensely in the shifting levels presented on stage. The result is a communal celebration of the personal resolution possible for each of the spectators, and comedy is instrumental in achieving this dynamic response to the familiar biblical narrative.

Notes

[1] Joseph Matthews Manly, Specimens of the Pre-Shakespearean Drama, (1897; rpt. New York: Biblo and Tannen, 1967).

[2] Joseph Quincy Adams, Chief Pre-Shakespearean Dramas (Boston: Houghton Mifflin Company, 1924).

[3] O.B. Hardison, Jr., Christian Rite and Christian Drama (Baltimore: The Johns Hopkins Press, 1965), pp. 1-34.

[4] E.K. Chambers, The Mediaeval Stage, 2 vols. (London: Oxford University Press, 1903).

[5] W.W. Greg, Bibliographical and Textual Problems of the English Miracle Cycles (London: Alexander Moring Limited, 1914), pp. 5-16.

[6] Albert Croll Baugh, "The Beginnings of the Drama," in A Literary History of England (New York: Appleton-Century-Crofts, Inc., 1948), I, 274.

[7] Baugh, p. 276.

[8] Frederik T. Wood, "The Comic Elements in the English Mystery Plays," Neophilologus, 25 (1940), 40.

[9] For similar emphasis on evolution, see Hardin Craig, English Religious Drama of the Middle Ages, (1955; rpt. London: Oxford University Press, 1967); and William G. McCollom, "From Dissonance to Harmony," The Theatre Annual, 21 (1964), 69-96.

[10] George R. Coffman, "A Plea for the Study of the Corpus Christi Plays as Drama," Studies in Philology, 26 (1929), 412.

[11] Coffman, p. 420.

[12] Charles Mills Gayley, Plays of Our Forefathers (1907; rpt. New York: Biblo and Tannen, 1968); and Samuel B. Hemingway, English Nativity Plays (1901; rpt. New York: Russell & Russell, 1964). It is noteworthy that both of these studies were re-

printed as late as the 1960s.

[13] Baugh, p. 281.

[14] Baugh, p. 281.

[15] Homer A. Watt, "The Dramatic Unity of the 'Secunda Pastorum'," in Essays and Studies in Honor of Carleton Brown (New York: New York University Press, 1940), pp. 158-66.

[16] Francis J. Thompson, "Unity in The Second Shepherds' Tale," Modern Language Notes, 64 (1949), 302.

[17] Robert C. Cosbey, "The Mak Story and Its Folklore Analogues," Speculum, 20 (1945), 317.

[18] E. Catherine Dunn, "Lyrical Form and the Prophetic Principle in the Towneley Plays," Mediaeval Studies, 23 (1961), 80-90. Dunn asserts that the unifying theme is the development of a prophetic principle in the plays. The Old Testament patriarchs--Adam, Noah, Abraham, and Moses--are presented as prophets, so that these plays form a unified theme that is expanded upon in the Processus prophetarum.

[19] William M. Manly, "Shepherds and Prophets: Religious Unity in the Towneley Secunda Pastorum," PMLA, 78 (1963), 151.

[20] Manly, p. 152.

[21] Manly, p. 153.

[22] Linda E. Marshall, "'Sacral Parody' in the Secunda Pastorum," Speculum, 47 (1972), 734.

[23] Maynard Mack, Jr., "The Second Shepherds' Play: A Reconsideration," PMLA, 93 (1978), 78-85.

[24] Mack, p. 83.

[25] Rose A. Zimbardo, "Comic Mockery of the Sacred," Educational Theatre Journal, 30 (1978), 398-406.

[26] Josie P. Campbell, "Farce as Function in the Wakefield Shepherds' Plays," Chaucer Review, 14 (1980), 336-43.

[27] Campbell, p. 342.

[28] Timothy Fry, O.S.B., "The Unity of the Ludus Coventriae," Studies in Philology, 48 (1951), 527-70; and Wood.

[29] Louis Cazamian, The Development of English Humour (New York: The Macmillan Company, 1930), pp. 74-75.

[30] Beatrice White, "Medieval Mirth," Anglia, 78 (1960),

293.

[31] See, for example, Thomas N. Grove, "Light in Darkness: The Comedy of the York 'Harrowing of Hell' as Seen Against the Backdrop of the Chester 'Harrowing of Hell'," _Neuphilologische Mitteilungen_, 75 (1974), 115-25.

[32] V.A. Kolve, _The Play Called Corpus Christi_ (Stanford, California: Stanford University Press, 1966), p. 139.

[33] Kolve, p. 12. See also Harry Levin, "From Play to Plays: The Folklore of Comedy," _Comparative Drama_, 16 (1982), 130-31.

[34] Kolve, pp. 23-25. See also R.W. Hanning, "'You Have Begun a Parlous Pleye': The Nature and Limits of Dramatic Mimesis as a Theme in Four Middle English 'Fall of Lucifer' Cycle Plays," _Comparative Drama_, 7 (1973), 22-23.

[35] Kolve, p. 32.

[36] Martin Stevens, "Illusion and Reality in the Medieval Drama," _College English_, 32 (1971), 455.

[37] Merle Fifield, "Quod quaeritis, o discipuli," _Comparative Drama_, 5 (1971), 57.

[38] Claude Gauvin, "Rite et jeu dans le theatre religieux anglais du Moyen Age," _Revue d'Histoire du Theatre_, 29 (1977), 140.

[39] Gayley, pp. 145-46.

[40] Clifford Davidson, "The Realism of the York Realist and the York Passion," _Speculum_, 50 (1975), 282.

[41] Davidson, p. 283.

[42] Kolve, p. 128.

[43] Margery M. Morgan, "'High Fraud': Paradox and Double-Plot in the English Shepherds' Plays," _Speculum_, 39 (1964), 676.

[44] "The Woman Taken in Adultery," in _Ludus Coventriae_, ed. K.S. Block (1922; rpt. Early English Text Sociey, e.s. 120, London: Oxford University Press, 1974), ll. 38, 41. Subsequent references from the N-Town cycle shall to be this edition and cited by line numbers in parentheses.

[45] John 8:6 states only that they sought Christ's counsel as a means of "tempting him, that they might have to accuse him." The N-Town playwright, interested in intellectual developments only faintly suggested in Scripture, used the reference as an opportunity for comic expansion and inquiry into the human

possibilities of such an undercurrent. Usually sober and devotional in tone, the N-Town cycle nevertheless makes full use of such opportunities.

CHAPTER 2:
Old Testament Challenges to Authority

The first plays of the extant Corpus Christi cycles attempt to define the human problem of recognizing divine authority and forming a response to it. These plays devote much attention to the opposing forces between which man is placed: God, according to the Old Testament image, is remote and omnipotent; Lucifer is base and wily. More importantly, however, the plays dealing with Creation, Cain and Abel, and Noah emphasize the active struggle man undergoes in recognizing and obeying divine authority, for the action played out in the central area of the stage closely parallels the lives of the spectators. How the struggle is resolved on stage decides for each character whether his passage through hell-mouth may be reversed in the harrowing of hell, and the members of the audience recognize that a similar polarity exists for them. The successful playwright involves his audience in such a process of recognition and evaluation through his use of comedy as a dramatic and theologic device.

In each of the plays, comic representation is most obvious for the characters who are traditionally evil: Lucifer, Cain, and Noah's wife. One notices, however, that virtuous characters are not spared; in fact, Abel and Noah are even mocked _because_ of their virtue. It seems clear, then, that the playwrights want their audiences to dispense with traditional alliances with good characters and to see the same stories from a different perspective. Doing so is a risky proposition, for it forces into the spectator's mind questions that may not have arisen independently. If these questions of faith are not resolved, then the spectator leaves the play with more doubt and confusion than before. If, on the other hand, the playwright is able to keep the audience involved in the action--so that the dramatic resolution is also a personal resolution of faith--then the audience is able to sense, as well as to know, the "rightness" of its conclusion. And in these plays, the comic presentations of confusion about authority and mixtures of divine and human levels of meaning sustain that involvement to work out three distinct tenets of a complex theological argument: the order imposed by Creation; the absoluteness of that order and man's recognition of it; and man's obligation to God, as a result of Creation.

Creation

At the heart of the plays about Creation is a sense of the order imposed on the universe. The opening of each play develops the implications of divine power inherent in God's statement, "Ego sum alpha et o." If one considers that these first speeches were useful in quieting the crowds as well as setting the theme and tone,[1] an opening declaration--like the following which begins the York Barkers' play--would be given added force and dignity by the booming voice of the actor:

> I am gracyus and grete, god withoutyn begynnyng,
> I am maker vnmade, all mighte es in me,
> I am lyfe and way vnto welth wynnyng,
> I am formaste and fyrste, als I byd sall it be.[2]

The strong sentence pattern that is repeated in these lines immediately establishes God as the central figure, the powerful force through which heaven and earth are created. Similar repetition in the Chester Tanners' play also serves to emphasize the absoluteness of the power of God: "It is my will it shoulde be soe; / hit is, yt was, it shalbe thus."[3] But in the cycle plays, the medieval playwrights attempt more than a visual representation of God's might:[4] they understand that the act of creation necessarily forces a relationship between a creature and its maker.

Even before the actual Creation begins, the Towneley dramatist clarifies this relationship by suggesting that the very existence of a thing depends on God's having thought of it and given it life:

> All maner thyng is in my thoght,
> Withoutten me ther may be noght,
> ffor all is in my sight;
> hit shall be done after my will,
> that I haue thought I shall fulfill
> And manteyn with my myght.[5]

A similar idea of divine control over the things and beings God creates is echoed in the N-Town play of the Creation:

> And all þat evyr xal haue beynge
> it is closyd in my mende
> whan it is made at my lykynge
> I may it saue I may it shende
> After my plesawns
> So gret of myth is my pouste
> All thyng xal be wrowth be me.
> (5-11)

This explicit reminder to the audience of divine power and control is useful to the playwright, for he then requires that the spectators view the Creation as a specific demonstration of might and skill.

The Towneley dramatist, in particular, does not allow the

audience to be diverted from this central idea: as he parts darkness from light, God reminds the spectators that "It shall be as I say; / after my will this is furth broght" (27-28). Water is separated from earth "bi oure assent" (31), and the creation of vegetation on the third day is interrupted with another reminder: "This is done after my will" (46). Therefore, one is encouraged to see the entire unfolding of the universe as the full development of God's plan for order,[6] a plan which begins, logically, with heaven and establishes decreasing levels of importance and strength to all the beings below. It follows that even the highest rank of angels has a certain debt to its creator, as these parallel passages from York and N-Town state:

> Baynely in my blyssyng I byd at here be
> A blys al-beledande abowte me;
> In þe whilke blys I byde at be here
> Nyen ordres of aungels full clere,
> In louyng ay lastande at lowte me.
>
> (York, 20-24)

> In hevyn I bylde Angell fful bryth
> my servauntys to be and for my sake
> with merth and melody worchepe my myth
> I belde them in my blysse
> Aungell in hevyn evyr more xal be
> In lyth ful clere bryth as ble
> With myrth and song to worchip me
> Of joye þei may not mys.
>
> (N-Town, 32-39)

In these passages, the audience is told directly the conditions of the relationship between God and the angels he created: they can share in the bliss of heaven only if they recognize God's might and worship him. Therefore, the playwrights here--and by implication in Towneley and Chester--subtly stress that God's benevolence is not without its price. Instead of a full devel-

35

opment of this idea, the skillful dramatists quickly present Lucifer and the first act of rebellion against God. Critic R.W. Hanning explains this shift in situation as a movement toward a more dramatic situation, for God's absence--a theological absurdity, but a dramatic necessity--alters the perspective of reality:

> With the withdrawal of God, we are asked to imagine the world not as it appears to the eye of faith--a place of order, testifying to God's rule, eliciting songs of praise--but as it is experienced by its creatures, as a place present-ing opportunities and challenges to control it as much as we can, as a place moreover in which to attempt to realize ourselves as fully as possi-ble. In such a place agon, irony, suspense, and peripateia become available to the dramatist--and the spectator--as they are not in heaven with God in residence.[7]

The timing of this shift in perspective is critical in achieving dramatic involvement of the audience, for the comic presentation of one who dares to challenge the established order builds interest in an important theme of the Old Testament plays.

Although all four of the cycle dramatists present Lucifer in vivid and human detail, the Towneley playwright is particu-larly adept at using colorful, comic characterization not as an end in itself but as a means of engaging the audience in the action on stage. Before Lucifer speaks, the angels praise God for all the beauty that he has created, and especially for Lucifer, who has brought them much joy:

> He is so lufly and so bright
> It is grete ioy to se that sight;
> We lofe the, lord, with all oure thoght,
> that sich thyng can make of noght.
> (73-76)

Because the audience knows the Genesis story, this statement becomes an ironic preparation for the entrance of the brightest angel. The spectators then anticipate the contrast to this image that they know the characterization of Lucifer will bring.

From the moment he begins to speak, Lucifer commands the attention of the audience. With playful audacity, he restates the fact of his beauty and brightness, addressing the spectators directly: "If that ye will behold me right, / this mastre longys to me" (80-81). This emphasis on subjective perception is sustained throughout the scene that follows, for there--depending on how one looks at it--Lucifer is successful in imitating God. Like the bold opening speeches of the Creation plays, Lucifer's proud declarations of power reverberate with self-confidence:

> Agans my grete myght
> may [no]thyng stand [ne] be.
> And ye well me behold
> I am a thowsand fold
> brighter then is the son;
> my strengthe may not be told,
> my myght may no thyng kon

(85-91)

The mere proximity of this speech to those made by God shows the clear parallel in tone and message, one that, in this fast-paced play, the spectators would not fail to notice. In many ways, Lucifer does seem like God, as he struts about the playing area declaring the absolute power that he believes he has. But the question that remains in the minds of the spectators is whether an assertion of might actually makes someone mighty, and this apparent power is contrasted sharply with the real power of God.[8]

One source of humor in the play is the emphasis given to appearances and imitation, and the subsequent inability of Lucifer and the other angels to see these deceptions for what they are. Lucifer asks a question that is intended to be rhetorical: "In heuen, therfor, wit I wold / Above me who shuld won" (92-93). The audience knows, however, that the answer to the question is "God," and immediately comic irony is established between what the character thinks he knows and what the audience knows as fact. This irony is emphasized and developed in the following scene through the dramatist's wordplay with semys, semely, and seme. Lucifer first uses the word in the sense of beauty and appropriateness, as he asserts to the angels that he will take God's throne:

> And ye shall se, full sone onone,
> How that me semys to sit in trone
>   as kyng of blis;
> I am so semely, blode & bone,
>   my sete shall be ther as was his.
>
> (99-103)

The humor in such an audacious speech is that Lucifer is much more semely (as opposed to actually) than he knows. Even as he seats himself in the throne, he is self-deceived to think his beauty makes him equal to the Trinity; in lines such as these, the audience is reminded of the confusion that can result from trusting appearances:

> Say, felows, how semys now me
> To sit in seyte of trynyte?
> I am so bright of ich a lym
> I trow me seme as well as hym.
>
> (104-07)

This passage reveals, Hanning suggests, that Lucifer "is not just mimicking; he is setting his will against God's."[9] How an angel reacts to such a declaration immediately classifies him as a _bonus angelus_ or a _malus angelus_, for the bad angels are drawn to trust appearances, whereas the good angels contrast the appropriateness of this deception to the reality of the divine plan of order. Continued repetition of the word _seme_ keeps this contrast at the center of the action, so that the audience recognizes this first rebellion as an active challenge to, and an indirect affirmation of, the power that Creation establishes.

The medieval audience would not, of course, have been lured, even with such witty and lively presentation, to take Lucifer's side in this struggle against a fixed order. Instead the play lends itself to the kind of appreciation for villainy that one sees in melodrama. Because they see Lucifer preen and boast,[10] the spectators are encouraged to view the flight from heaven to hell as a deserved, fitting resolution to the action. The audience is then involved in the drama, even if no association with the character is founded. This intense involvement causes the spectators to keep the theme of the play--God's order of the universe--as an appropriate backdrop to the scenes that follow.

This involvement, sustained through comedy, also creates a dramatic tension, for the irony of appearances becomes vivid. The Creation plays establish physical _loci_ for heaven and hell, including both the vivid symbols and the less tangible presentations of bliss and anguish that one is likely to find there.[11]

Because, as one critic suggests, these symbols of one's possible destination remain on stage throughout the cycle,[12] the audience is always confronted with the polarities of God's plan. In such a situation, tension is likely to result, in spite of what _seems_ to be the condition in the central, middle-earth portion of the playing area. Similarly, a contrast develops in the minds of the spectators between what they know to be the right attitude and what seems to be logical. As soon as a human is represented on stage, this essential tension increases.

Although the leaves containing the Temptation and Fall of man are missing from the Towneley manuscript, one may surmise that there, as in the other cycles, the basic question is the same: what is real, and what is illusion? Even though, for example, Eve knows that God has forbidden her to eat fruit from the tree of life, she still has difficulty deciding whether God or Satan has told her the truth. In the York Cowpers' play, she asks Satan, "Is þis soth þat þou sais?" (74), indicating that she does not believe that God had told her the truth about the effects of the fruit. Adam, too, is easily swayed to dismiss the warning from God and to suspect him of creating deception for the purpose of keeping them subservient. As opposed to the dramatic treatment of Lucifer, where even in Chester the bright angel mimics God enthroned (185-93), the scenes depicting man's Fall are lifeless, with slow pacing and flat characterization.

Most criticism stresses the stasis of these plays by focusing on such elements as typology and metaphor.[13] What energizes these scenes, however, is the thematic continuation of such a contrast in the context of man's situation. The audience laughs at Lucifer's downfall because he is so blatantly rebellious, in spite of the fact that his direct knowledge of heavenly bliss should have restrained him. But Adam and Eve seem to be more like victims than willful deceivers, for they are pitted against two extremes, and the playwrights focus on their difficulty in recognizing which extreme—good or evil—is truly powerful, and which is simply an illusion.

The comic presentation of Lucifer's disobedience is therefore turned on its head when the audience sees itself in a similar situation. Remembering the questions about established order that are posed humorously in the scenes of the fall of angels, the spectators cease laughing when they see the human consequences that result when one fails to perceive the divine order as it exists. The intensity of the involvement continues, although changed, and prepares the audience for the next scenes: the presentation of Cain and Abel.

Cain and Abel

In the cycle plays of Cain and Abel, the rebellion of the preceding plays offers a different dramatic possibility, for in several respects the position of the audience is similar to the relationship that Cain and Abel have with God. First, the human situation is paralleled closely on stage in that the brothers have only second-hand knowledge of God. Just as the spectators must rely on faith and the words of their predecessors to understand and accept God's authority, Cain and Abel must trust the advice generated by the example of their parents.[14] Second, the dramatic situation is more interesting because it offers a fairer context for a struggle: Cain and Abel have more knowledge, and therefore more choices, than their parents.

Particularly in the Chester Drapers' play, where the creation of the world, fall of man, and slaying of Abel are compressed into one play, thematic connection is established between the early Genesis presentations. Hints of staging in the N-Town cycle indicate that the first four plays may have been presented in sequence.[15] Even in York and Towneley, where the plays appear distinct from one another, the conditions of Creation echo through the later plays. The Cain and Abel story, presented in such a context, thus becomes a dynamic testing of divine order, in which human doubts and resolutions are pitted against a distant and impenetrable authority.

The human approach of the play is evident most notably in the presentation of Cain, for he is a character whom the audience knows well. The servant, Garcio, in the <u>Mactacio Abel</u> makes this association for the audience even before Cain appears on stage:

> Gedlyngis, I am a fulle grete wat,
> A good yoman my master hat,
> fful well ye all hym ken;
> Begyn he with you for to stryfe,
> certis, then mon ye neuer thryfe.
>
> (14-18)

In essence, Garcio here identifies his master as a stock character, a type of person whom each spectator has had to endure in his daily existence. The association that is established therefore puts the spectators in the position of the servant and asks them to perceive Cain as a menacing master. This opening speech is double-edged, however, for it also introduces the central character as a type for someone quite removed from humanity: the devil.

By the time the mystery cycles were written, Hebrew tradition and rabbinical lore had long since established the legend of Cain's descendance from the devil.[16] The cycle playwrights use this legend as an integral part of the characterization of Cain, an association that the audience would recognize easily. In this sense, Cain becomes a type of the evil character who rebels against God and despairs of his forgiveness.[17] In the Mactacio Abel, this connection is made by the servant Garcio—also called Pike-harnes—in his opening address to the audience:

> Bot I trow, bi god on life,
> Som of you ar his men.
> Bot let youre lippis couer youre ten,
>   harlottis, euerichon!

(19-22)

This curious passage goes beyond warning the spectators not to smile. John Gardner convincingly argues that the speaker is referring to the pointed teeth which are characteristic of devils, and which many members of the audience must be careful to conceal.[18] Thus, this reference underlines two basic assertions: Satan is not simply an historical figure, and many in the audience are his servants, not God's. Such a declaration immediately forces the picture of Cain to become more complex than a one-dimensional type, for the audience has already been placed in the uncomfortable position of not knowing how to react to him. And the first glimpse of Cain reinforces such confusion.

After the tension caused by Garcio's speech, the audience laughs with relief at the Wakefield Master's presentation of Cain as a plowman. The unique depiction of Cain as a simple farmer struggling for dominance over his team is, in itself, a welcome source of laughter, one that a skilled actor would use to full advantage. Even the exclamations and repetition of monosyllabic words in this opening passage suggest enormous comic possibilities, as one imagines Cain's grunting, sweating, and shoving to control the stubborn beasts:

> Io furth, greyn-horne! and war oute, gryme!
> Drawes on! god gif you ill to tyme!
> Ye stand as ye were fallen in swyme;
> What! will ye no forther, mare?
> War! let me se how down will draw;
> Yit, shrew, yit, pull on a thraw!
> What! it semys for me ye stand none aw!
> I say, donnyng, go fare!
> A, ha! god gif the soro & care!

(25-33)

Members of the audience laugh at the humiliation of Cain, at his inability to maintain this basic principle of order that his position as farmer directs. Over-reaction on Cain's part, accomplished surely—as his speech suggests—through exaggerated facial expressions and gestures, involves the spectators in the action and entices them to see in this rogue a buffoon that they have met before—not entirely the personification of evil that Garcio's opening address suggests. Cain is certainly the bad plowman that Jeffrey finds him to be, an inversion of the Christian icon of the obedient servant presented both in scripture and in medieval literature.[19] Immediately, the contrast between

Cain and other plowmen--for example, the Parson's companion in the _Canterbury Tales_--is evident to the audience; yet this comic deflation of the ideal serves to involve rather than alienate the spectators. Despite the fact that Cain is clearly associated with evil and that his struggle with plowing parallels his struggle to serve the right master, the audience is drawn to him and sees in his situation an exaggerated representation of its own confusion about divine authority.

Just as the established order seems to fail for Cain in his mastery over his plowing team, it also becomes inverted in his relationship with his boy. Brewbarret in the fragmented York _Sacrificium Cayme and Abell_ is possibly only mischievous, but the portrait drawn by the Wakefield Master shows a direct challenge to authority in the first dialogue between Cain and Pikeharnes. The boy responds when called by his master, but his attitude is insolent and daring. He curses Cain instead of greeting him, and Cain's response is astonishment:

> _Cayn_. How! pike-harnes, how! com heder belife!
> _Garcio_. I fend, godis forbot, that euer thou
>   thrife!
> _Cayn_. What, boy, shal I both hold and drife?
>   heris thou not how I cry?
>
>   (37-40)

Especially because the audience has just witnessed a physical struggle for control in the plowing scene, this wrangling evokes humor in its repetition of Cain's predicament. The frustration and despair that Cain feels with his plowing team resound in this opening dialogue and lead inevitably to the challenge to fight. The plowman, in his toiling and arguing, struggles several times to affirm the nature of the master-servant relationship. He calls Garcio "boy" twice and eventually gives a direct reminder to the servant of his inferior position: "I am thi master" (50). To the spectators, this puffing of stature is ironic and comic, for instead of revealing the speaker's power, the statement in its context shows Cain's lack of control.

One therefore sees in the Mactacio Abel an initial presentation of the first murderer that differs significantly from treatments in the other cycles.[20] He is not, at first, simply angry and selfish, as the York Cain, who asserts that he "wille wyrke euen as I will" (53). Nor is he initially adamant in his attitudes toward tithing, like the N-Town depiction of him. Instead, the first sketch of Cain that the Wakefield dramatist outlines is as a struggling plowman whose nature may not, under different circumstances, be so unlike the characters of many members of the audience. Dorrel T. Hanks, Jr., explains this characterization in terms of its allegorical significance to the audience:

> Cain, to be sure, is a villain, but the audience must have seen him as the villain we all carry under our skins. Abel's constant virtue is irritating, the tithe is onerous, crops do fail and lead farmers to question Providence. Cain is then almost as much Everyman as murderer.[21]

Although Hanks exaggerates and oversimplifies this parallel without developing its implications in the play, he points to an immense achievement on the part of the Wakefield Master: the dramatist places before his spectators the possibility that Cain was a person like many of them. Establishing such a connection works well for dramatic purposes; for, in addition to suspending the usual reaction of the audience toward an evil character, this association prepares the spectators to respond on several levels to Abel's entrance in the next scene.

The intimations of the theme of the Mactacio Abel--recognition and testing of authority--are first brought to their full comic and dramatic potential in the scenes that present the conflict between Cain and Abel. As Abel enters the stage area, the members of the audience are ready to witness a brawl between Cain and his servant. The interruption of the fight leaves Cain with fists and emotions raised; and even before Cain responds to Abel's standard benediction with "Com kis myne ars" (59), the audience knows that he will channel his anger and frustrations into his treatment of Abel. There is delight for the spectators in both the anticipation and the comic unfolding of their argument. Cain, at last, has found an inferior who appears to be weaker than he, and he takes full advantage of the position that he assumes is his right.

Cain reminds both Abel and the audience of his superiority not, as in Chester (529), by a direct statement, "I am the elder of us too," but by using with Abel the tone that he had intended to use in his address to Garcio. Thus he says haughtily to Abel, "Thou shuld haue bide til thou were cald" (61); and his barrage of insults that follow reinforces his harsh bid for superiority:

> Com nar, & other drife or hald,
> and kys the dwillis toute.

          Go grese thi shepe vnder the toute,
          ffor that is the moste lefe.

                                                          (62-65)

The reference here to "drife or hald" echoes Cain's earlier

struggles with his mare and servant, and one sees that, in this

situation, he is resolved to keep the upper hand. More notice-

able to the medieval audience and to the modern reader, however,

are the blatant scatological remarks Cain makes.[22] Eleanor

Prosser's reaction to passages like this in the Mactacio Abel is

to caution critics not to accept such vulgarity in the plays as

part of medieval devotion:

> We have come to realize--and one reads this in
> almost all recent studies of English religious
> drama--that to medieval man, religion encompassed
> all of life, its moments of awe, its staggering
> horrors, even its idiotic jokes. This attitude
> is so foreign to us that . . . we may have swung
> too far in our determination to be tolerant. We
> seem to believe that since humor and vulgarity
> could be consonant with true devotion, therefore
> we must accept any and all humor, and even ob-
> scenity for obscenity's sake, as being completely
> in harmony with medieval religion.[23]

Certainly, one must agree that Cain's advice to Abel does

not even slightly resemble a prayer, and to call it "devotional"

would be ludicrous. But to dismiss the entire play on the basis

that the playwright could not control his vulgarity, as Prosser

implies, is to make several critical errors. The first of these

is to assume that the medieval audience--and the playwright

himself--did not find Cain's curses shocking and offensive. The

second--and more critical--error is to refuse to see a dramatic

purpose in stunning the audience this way.

     To a medieval audience, prepared to witness a Corpus

Christi cycle, intrusion of base humor in this scene was likely to produce results similar to what happens in modern gatherings: surprise, tense laughter, and strong involvement with the stage action. If one considers, for example, the use of obscenities by modern comedians, one recognizes the humorous effects of coarse language. In many cases, the source of humor is the impassivity of the comedian as he utters into a microphone the most vulgar words of our language. Part of the humor lies in the shock of the words themselves, and part in the ease of delivery to a large, mixed audience. Evidence for similar comic effect in the Mactacio Abel is the way in which Cain interjects such obscenities into the context of a conversation about one's debt to God. Abel's deadpan, conventional responses merely bolster the comic and dramatic strength of Cain's utterances, and the audience becomes involved in their banter, nervously and eagerly awaiting the next blow from Cain.

Cain's attitudes toward tithing and toward God are as shocking to the audience as his language, for his rebellion and coarseness seem natural traits of his character. Instead of revealing Cain as a vindictive man who is determined to humiliate his brother, the argument between Cain and Abel becomes a comic vehicle through which these attitudes are highlighted. Abel, whom Prosser describes as "a stuffed shirt" and "pompous do-gooder,"[24] presents his pious argument to convince Cain of his obligation to God and of his need to tithe properly. He fails to do so, however, and some critics imply a carelessness on the part of the playwright for allowing Abel to be so feeble:

"Doubtless this [characterization] was very naughty of the dramatist, and a desertion of his didactic duty, especially as Abel is an acknowledged ante-type of Christ, and his death a prefiguring of the Passion."[25]

Although this portrayal does weaken the traditional presentation of virtue, it is, I suggest, meant to cause a reaction. For the insipidness of Abel fulfills a very important dramatic function: his rehearsed logic baits Cain to challenge--playfully, at first--several aspects of faith. The compact dialogue not only introduces the subject of the sacrifice and shows the differences in the brothers' attitudes; it also illustrates Cain's ability to extract cues from Abel's speeches and twist them into a form of rebellion against the ideas:

> Abell. Caym, leife this vayn carpyng,
> ffor god giffys the all thi lifyng.
> Cayn. Yit boroed I neuer a farthyng,
> of hym, here my hend.
> Abell. Brother, as elders haue vs kend,
> ffirst shuld we tend with oure hend,
> and to his lofying sithen be brend.
>
> Cayn. My farthyng is in the preest hand
> syn last time I offyrd.

(97-105)

These stylized urgings of Abel offer a challenge for Cain to shock his brother and invert his argument; and he meets that challenge by leading the debate to a conclusion that Abel never intended. Cain plays with the word hand, using it in several contexts to trace the deterioration of the image of Christian sacrifice. He teasingly ignores the description of the benevolent hand of God, who "giffys the all thi lifyng," and the hand of the faithful servant who gladly offers a sacrifice. He reduces the image--and the relationship between God and man--to its most pejorative sense: a businessman's emphasis on debt and repayment. The concluding development of this passage, an anachronistic criticism of the corruption of church tithing, is surely not what Abel intended Cain to derive from his speech, and it--like the crude language--surprises and delights the audience.

The members of the audience can appreciate this feigned naivete on the part of Cain because they know, just as he does, the literal meaning of Abel's words. Like Cain, they know that to assume an actual business relationship with God is ridiculous, but they enjoy the word play of the quick action on stage. If Abel were to continue in the same argument, Cain could maintain this stance as devil's advocate, trying to agitate his brother and distort his logic. Abel changes the subject, however, and in doing so is even more irritating to Cain than he was before. Cain's playfulness then shifts suddenly, for his games of questioning become more serious:

> We! wherof shuld I tend, leif brothere?
> ffor I am ich yere wars then othere,
> here my trouth it is none othere;
> My wynnyngis ar bot meyn,
> No wonder if that I be leyn;
> ffull long till hym I may me meyn,
> ffor bi hym that me dere boght,
> I traw that he will leyn me noght.
>
> (108-15)

Although comic irony is evident in some of these lines--one doubts, for example, that Cain is as frail and lean as line 112 implies--the overall tone is more serious than earlier passages. For instance, he questions the value of "spiritual rent," turning the parable of the talents, as one critic suggests, into a verbal exercise.[26] The logic to support religious doubts, however, is based on more than word play. Cain looks at the hard life he is "blessed" with and wonders why he has to be thankful at all. When Abel offers this inappropriate comfort, "godis grace is bot a lone" (117), the amusement with which Cain might have responded earlier is replaced with a much more serious literal development of the figure of speech:

> Lenys he me, as com thrift apon the so?
> ffor he has euer yit beyn my fo;
> ffor had he my freynd beyn,
> Other gatis it had beyn seyn.
> When all mens corn was fayre in feld
> Then was myne not worth a neld;
> When I shuld saw, & wantyd seyde,
> And of corn had full grete neyde,
> Then gaf me none of his,
> No more will I gif hym of this.
> hardely hold me to blame
> bot if I serue hym of the same.
>
> (118-29)

Cain here questions God's authority by examining the implications of the business relationship that he interpreted from Abel's comment. His first point, that things are progressively deteriorating, is a convincing reminder to the audience of the difficulties that many of them face in life.[27] And for Cain, God's failure to meet his contractual obligation offers humans the freedom to do the same.

Reciprocity is not the basis of God's plan, however, and the audience always knows this; nevertheless, identification with and sympathy for Cain prevent the spectators from deprecating him. In the middle section of the play, then, the audience is in the uneasy position of wanting both a positive resolution for Cain (even though biblical history is against them) and a strong reassurance that their principles of faith are sound. Critics vary in their assessments of the focus of this middle section, but most consider it very serious, as opposed to the farcical opening and closing.[28] If one considers the dramatic advantage of using comedy when the audience is already in emotional tumult, then the text provides evidence that the spectators find a welcome relief in the persistence of Cain's antics, a relief that paradoxically brings them closer to the heart of the play.

Part of this comedy, as well as the dramatic action, stems from the limited characterization of Abel, who is certainly no match for his brother. The "sermonyng" (86) that he offers as solution to Cain's questions is comic in its lack of substance: his only comment after Cain criticizes God for being unequitable is "Leif brother, say not so" (130). Hartnett points to a problem faced by all dramatists who try to present virtuous characters: "it is difficult . . . to endow saintly people with vivid humanity, because they live in complete harmony with human and divine sanction."[29] Yet, in spite of this appreciation for the difficulty of the playwright's task, Hartnett herself succumbs to her distaste for Abel when she calls him "a relentless nag" who is "invariably and almost intolerably right." She surmises that the spectators would share these feelings, for they would associate Abel with "preachers who delivered a similar message with irritating regularity."[30]

This pious scolding intensifies as the conflict between

them develops, but it never changes the focus of the scene. Always the attention is directed toward Cain: his speeches are longer, more original, and more animated. Although Prosser doubts that the playwright means to satirize Abel,[31] the marked disparity in their prayers of sacrifice indicates a clear shift of attention away from Abel. In these passages, Abel's cloying meekness is weak in its juxtaposition to the lively prayer made by Cain:

> <u>Abell</u>. God that shope both erth and heuen,
> I pray to the thou here my steven,
> And take in thank, if thi will be,
> the tend that I offre here to the;
> ffor I gif it in good entent
> to the, my lord, that all has sent.
> I bren it now, with stedfast thoght,
> In worship of hym that all has wroght.
>   <u>Cayn</u>. Ryse! let me now, syn thou has done;
> lord of heuen, thou here my boyne!
> And ouer, godis forbot, be to the
> thank or thew to kun me;
> ffor, as browke I thise two shankys,
> It is full sore, myne vnthankys,
> The teynd that I here gif to the,
> of corn, or thyng, that newys me;
> Bot now begyn will I then,
> syn I must nede my tend to bren.

> (174-91)

The conventional soft rhymes and lulling rhythm of the first prayer are drowned out by the unusual and laughable sounds of such words as <u>shankys</u> and <u>vnthankys</u>, resulting in a subtle mockery of the reverence itself as well as its expression.[32] Thus, in spite of the fact that Abel's attitude is the "proper," "appropriate" one, the whole movement of the scene is comic: Cain's lively retorts command more attention than the religious rhetoric which prompted them.

The scene builds in intensity to the humorous miscounting

of the sheaves and Cain's subsequent irritation when Abel interrupts him with trite, self-righteous censure. The comic possibilities of the reluctant offering Cain makes urge a skilled actor to take command of the scene and involve the spectators fully. One can imagine an air of feigned innocence as the actor playing Cain pretends to be conscientious in his counting, all the while sharing a joke with the audience:

> Oone shefe, oone, and this makys two,
> bot nawder of thise may I forgo:
> Two, two, now this is thre,
> yei, this also shall leif with me:
> ffor I will chose and best haue,
> this hold I thrift of all this thrafe;
> Wemo, wemo, foure, lo, here!
> better groved me no this yere.
>
> (192-99)

Whereas in the N-Town play, Cain resolves stubbornly to "tythe þe werst" (97), the character portrayed by the Wakefield dramatist is engaged in a more prolonged debate with himself, as the passage shows. And the underlying belief--that one can close his eyes and pretend that the sacrifice was offered properly (225-28)--is both the comic and thematic development toward which the playwright has worked.

Such defiance is a game, since Cain knows that Abel's reminders of correct attitudes and procedures are the truth; yet the game is an amusing, interesting release, and the interjections of religious and moral truth are, at first, humorous because they are obvious enough to disclose that Abel misunderstands the rules of the game. Through this play he shares with the audience, Cain is able to implant serious ideas in the context of a farcical scene. For example, although his miscounting already reduces the size of his offering, he questions the value of offering corn of the highest quality. Cain's miserly suffering as he sacrifices is comic in such exaggerated lines as "It goyse agans myn hart full sore" (221), again a skillful turning of the spectators away from their established opinions of Cain and his sin. Only hints of Cain's inevitable destiny are present, and these are undeveloped.[33]

The surfeit of admonishment offered by Abel, then, represents a kind of high-level play with the "normal," pious--and therefore dull--warnings, such as "Caym, thou tendis wrang, and of the warst" (224). Abel even challenges Cain with an issue that is not on the surface of their discussion: "Came, of god me thynke thou has no drede" (233). The crude retort, although shocking both in the direct insult and in its ascription of human qualities to God, echoes the annoyance of the audience when confronted, at the height of their enjoyment, with such a severe, sanctimonious remark:

> Now and he get more, the dwill me spede!
> As mych as oone reepe,
> ffor that cam hym full light chepe;
> Not as mekill, grete ne small
> as he myght wipe his ars withall.
> ffor that, and this that lyys here,
> haue cost me full dere.
>
> (234-40)

Such a declaration presents the spectators with a glimpse of the extent of Cain's audacity and the fearlessness with which he challenges divine authority, but, more importantly, it elicits what Kolve calls "the vulgar laugh, the laugh from the belly rather than the smile."[34] In doing so, this level of comedy maintains the emotional involvement of the audience at a critical scene in the play. For while Cain's boldness—intensified by a scurrilous reference to God, not Abel, say, or Garcio—remains attractive to the spectators, they always possess certain knowledge of the fate of the murderer. As Cain rationalizes his manner of sacrifice, telling Abel, "How that I tend, rek the neuer a deill" (247), they know exactly where such reasoning leads: to murder and damnation. Ironically, however, they are drawn to participate in Cain's challenge, to test vicariously the questions that they dare not utter in their own lives.

Some critics interpret Cain only as a type of the devil or of Judas,[35] but to reduce in this way is to overlook one of the most skillful achievements of the Wakefield Master: the dynamism that exists, even in the printed text, between the character in conflict and his attentive audience. In its uneasy stance toward Cain, the audience is at its most vulnerable point and might readily respond to emotional appeals that strengthen the identification with him. The plowman's insistence on his misfortune and his apparent subjection to the whims of nature and a distant God remind the spectators that they, too, do not control their everyday existence as much as they would like. The implication, however, is even stronger: by promising obedience and ever looking beyond this world to the next, people often accept without question the hardships that they assume serve some divine purpose. Thus, concomitant with the humor visible in Abel's stock responses is an underlying frustration—to both

Cain and the audience--that logical answers do not exist.

A danger for the playwright is to leave these questions unresolved by heightening sympathy for Cain and substantiating Cain's claim that "God is out of hys wit" (300). And even in the tithing scene itself, the Wakefield Master manages to solve this problem by forcing the audience to realize, even if Cain does not, that the game is over. Cain shows signs of frustration as he assumes that his offering will be rejected, and his curt responses to Abel suggest that perhaps he is not enjoying the teasing as much as he did before. The following passage, for example, shows Cain lashing out at Abel as if in premonition that his offering will not burn:

> Abell. If thou teynd right thou mon it fynde.
> Cayn. Yei, kys the dwills ars behynde;
> The dwill hang the bi the nek!
> how that I teynd, neuer thou rek.
> Will thou not yit hold thi peasse?
> of this Ianglyng I reyde thou seasse,
> And teynd I well, or tend I ill,
> bere the euen & speke bot skill.
>
> (265-92)

Here is a difference from the earlier Cain, who challenged authority by asking questions about the obligations he and God have to each other. This passage shows Cain's lack of confidence in a feeble attempt to assert himself, to silence a voice that speaks the truth. The situational irony in this scene ends the game for the audience, since the hellish imagery in the text--and, conceivably, presented vividly on stage[36]--would serve to remind the spectators of the doom that awaits Cain:

> [Cayn] Bot now syn thou has teyndid thyne,
> Now will I set fyr on myne.
> We! out! haro! help to blaw!
> It will not bren for me, I traw;

>   Puf! this smoke dos me mych shame--
>   now bren, in the dwillys name!
>   A! what dwill of hell is it?
>   Almost had myne breth beyn dit.
>   had I blawen oone blast more
>   I had beyn choked right thore;
>   It stank like the dwill in hell,
>   that longer ther myght I not dwell.
>
>   (273-84)

Cain has a close call here, one that would remind the audience of the horrors of hell that await those who deliberately ignore their need to obey God. Although a skilled actor would draw laughter in this scene as he sputters and chokes in exaggeration, the serious implication of the stage action begins to balance the humor, slightly distancing the audience from Cain. The hostility that Cain exhibits toward Abel increases this distance, for it is at this point that pathos--a stance that differs greatly from identification with a character--intrudes on the presentation of Cain and turns the murder scene into the tragic, inevitable conclusion of a serious game.

What Woolf calls a "furious contempt for God"[37] in the N-Town Cain is not evident in the Wakefield characterization: instead, one sees a person who is pathetically stubborn, who lacks the sense to know when a joke is over. For example, when God speaks to Cain, offering a simple explanation of the reverence required of him, Cain responds not with repentance or even with a direct question--such as, why must it be so? or why have you made things difficult for me?--but with a jaunty remark that betrays his lack of confidence:

>   Deus. Cam, whi art thou so rebell
>   Agans thi brother abell?
>   Thar thou nowther flyte ne chyde,
>   if thou tend right thou gettis thi mede;

And be thou sekir, if thou teynd fals,
thou bese alowed ther after als. [Exit Deus.]
   Caym. Whi, who is that hob-ouer-the-wall?
we! who was that that piped so small?
Com go we hens, for perels all;
   God is out of hys wit.
(293-300)

Cain is uncertain in his humor here, as he tries to establish himself in the hierarchy of authority by scoffing at the power of God. He is immediately unsettled by his own pronouncement, telling Abel "on land then will I flyt" (303) and hoping to hide from God.

At this point in the play, the Wakefield Master once again models Cain more after human nature than after the biblical figure he portrays. A sign of guilt emerges in Cain's desire to hide, to go where ". . . god shall not me see" (307). Instead of bringing Cain to a direct admission of his fault, however, the dramatist has him act the way many people would: he blames Abel for his predicament. Cain should acknowledge openly his indebtedness to God; instead, he chooses to repay what he owes Abel. And, as this passage shows, the meaning of the debt is reduced to its purely earthly terms:

   Na, na, abide, we haue a craw to pull;
Hark, speke with me or thou go;
what! wenys thou to skape so?
we! na! I aght the a fowll dispyte,
and now is tyme that I hit qwite.
(311-15)

Here Cain's basic humanity--not pure villainy, as in other accounts--dominates his action. He reverts to his frustration as he realizes that his attempt to cheat God was futile, and the motive for the murder becomes a jealous response to the fact that God preferred Abel's sacrifice. Here, there is no display of cunning, as exhibited by the Chester Cain, who lures Abel away--presumably from the sight of God--and plans to kill him because he seeks "to passe mee of renowne" (602). In that cycle the murder is a direct challenge of maystry:

> Thoughe God stoode in this place
> for to helpe thee in this case,
> thou should dye before his face.
> Have this, and gett thee right!
>
> (613-16)

The Wakefield playwright takes a different perspective on the murder, for envy and anger motivate the crime, and Cain does not think of God as he kills Abel. He wants simply to quiet the "old shrew" (330) who has been nagging him.

Such comic development at the time of the murder reveals the interest of the Wakefield dramatist in sustaining audience involvement and focusing on the spectators' reactions. The insult echoed in Cain's generalized, compact statement, "So lig down ther and take thi rest, / thus shall shrewes be chastysed best" (326-27), would be likely to draw snickers from the audience--despite the fact that their stance toward Cain has been altered and that a horrible crime is occurring. There is also, as it were, almost a sense of relief that the whining, self-righteous answers Abel offers (such as "If thyne smoked am I to wite?" 322) will cease at last. The N-Town playwright makes no such appeal to his audience--inviting, instead, scorn for Cain and pity for Abel:

> þou xalt be ded I xal þe slo
> þi lord þi god þou xalt nevyr se
> Tythyng more xalt þou nevyr do
> with þis chavyl bon I xal sle þe

61

```
þi deth is dyht þi days be go
out of myn handys xalt þou not fle
With þis strok I þe kylle
Now þis boy is slayn and dede
Of hym I xal nevyr more han drede
He xal here after nevyr ete brede
With þis gresse I xal hym hylle.
```

(146-56)

The overkill in the expression of this passage is a more serious crime than the actual murder. The Wakefield dramatist, in contrast, is careful to avoid such easy alliances between the spectators and his characters, and he uses understatement rather than hyperbole to make his point.

An important turning point for the audience occurs after line 330: the direct address begun by Cain cuts short the laughter of those who see poetic justice in the murder and removes the smug sense of superiority from those who find his behavior abominable. He promises, "well wars then it is, / right so shall it be" (334-35), a reminder to the spectators of the heinous crimes in their own time. Implicit in this statement is not only a criticism of the intensity of the crimes humans are capable of inflicting, but also a suggestion that the crime is made more serious because although centuries of history have shown the effects of murder, people do not improve.

The text of the Mactacio Abel reveals that overt scolding, as a resolution to the play, is not the intention of the dramatist. After the intense emotional involvement it has formed with the character of Cain, the audience expects more than a shift to traditional preaching of established values. Whereas the Chester play of Cain and Abel ends abruptly after the murder, with the curse pronounced by God transforming Cain into a sinner "dampned without grace" (666), and the N-Town version closes the action with a remorseful, ashamed Cain seeking "Ffrom mannys ssyht me hyde" (195), the Towneley adaptation of the biblical account shows Cain to be consistent with the earlier characterization: stubborn, imperious, and damned. Once he overcomes his initial instinct to want death for himself and recognizes that "In hell I wote mon be my stall" (375), Cain recovers quickly and continues to manipulate language to clear himself of guilt--at least on a superficial level. This conclusion, a unique ending to the Cain story, is consistent with the rest of the play, not only in terms of characterization and dramatic unity; it also reveals the concern of the playwright that the spectators respond with intensity to the situation on stage.

Most noticeable to the audience is that Cain is unchanged by the important events of the play: he quickly shifts his attention from the spiritual implications of God's curse to the practical consideration of hiding Abel's body. He remains the brutish master, as he hits Pike-harnes and explains only ". . . I did it bot to vse my hand" (393). Although this section of the play, like the earlier scenes, attempts to humanize Cain by showing his dealing with guilt,[38] here the playwright more explicitly directs the attention of the spectators to the illogical arguments Cain puts forth, resulting in their laughing at his equivocation, his attempts--as one critic calls it--to "burn his corn and eat it too."[39] This attitude is consistent with his earlier perspective, for in explaining his logic to Abel, Cain discloses that to have it both ways Abel must "chaunge thi conscience, as I do myn" (263). Boone asserts that this line focuses on the difference in values of the brothers, supported in the play by the changing meaning of the word skill:

> The discourse of the play drives a wedge between "that which is reasonable" and that which is "proper, right, or just." It ascribes not merely different significations but different systems of signification, the material and spiritual, to what is split off on either side. To say of God "I did hym neuer yit bot skill" Cain must change his conscience so that it is oriented to the material and spiritual simultaneously, an impossible feat.[40]

Even though Cain fails in changing his conscience and has the opportunity to discover the futility in manipulating reason when an absolute hand controls what is "proper, right, and just," his inability to change from this early stance becomes comic. Whereas the debates with Abel direct the laughter of the spectators toward the simple, often incomprehensible answers provided by the pious younger brother, the strength of Garcio's sarcasm and the dramatist's shift to an easily recognized parody of legal procedures redirects this laughter toward Cain.

Because he accepts in direct terms the fact of his damnation, saying "Ordand ther is my stall, / with sathanas the feynd" (466-67), Cain then seeks to avoid earthly punishment, since--from the start of the play--he has assumed that spiritual redemption is impossible.[41] In the language and procedures of medieval law, Cain is given a context for this evasion.[42]

The terms of legal acquittal echoed by Cain establish the

64

rules for a new game to be played out on stage, and Garcio is prompted to act his part:

> Caym. Stand vp, my good boy, belife,
> and thaym peasse both man & [w]ife;
> And who so will do after me
> ffull slape of thrift then shal he be.
> Bot thou must be my good boy,
> and cry oyes, oyes, oy!
>
> (411-16)

The statements Garcio delivers to the spectators in the lines that follow assure that they enjoy this false pardon, delighting in the feeble attempt to use material, earthly means to acquit one of a primarily spiritual crime. The comic shifting of levels and undermining of Cain's argument through emphasis on his hypocrisy is evident in these lines:

> Caym. I commaund you in the kyngis nayme,
> Garcio. And in my masteres, fals Cayme,
> Caym. That no man at thame fynd fawt ne blame.
> Garcio. Yey, cold rost is at my masteres hame.
>
> Caym. Nowther with hym nor with his knafe,
> Garcio. What, I hope my master rafe.
> Caym. ffor thay ar trew, full many fold;
> Garcio. My master suppys no coyle bot cold.
> Caym. The kyng wrytis you vntill.
> Garcio. Yit ete I neuer half my fill.
>
> Caym. The kyng will that thay be safe,
> Garcio. Yey, a draght of drynke fayne wold I
>   hayfe.
> Caym. At thare awne will let tham wafe;
> Garcio. My stomak is redy to receyfe.
>
> (418-31)

The comedy evident in a creative delivery of these lines, as Cain stands in ignorance of the pronouncements which deflate him before the audience, moves the spectators to recognize, from a different perspective, the same question that was evident at the start of the play. Garcio's insistence on physical nourishment reminds the audience of the unswerving pragmatism of this pardon; in their laughter at this contradiction, the spectators become involved in an examination of both Cain's and their own refusal to accept the subservient role of earthly to spiritual concerns. Brockman offers this terse conjecture of the effect of this closing on the audience:

> Perhaps they would ponder the extent to which their society in fact corresponded to the City of Man displayed before them and take the theological implications quite seriously. Certainly the laughter greeting Cain's references to abuses of the law would be meaningful rather than meaningless laughter. [43]

On a dramatic, as well as theological, level, this laughter becomes meaningful, for it prevents the spectators from fostering their identification with and pity for Cain. Bacause of the danger in tempting the audience with thoughts of questioning absolute authority, the playwright needs, before the play is ended, to burst the bubble he has carefully blown. In the Mactacio Abel, Woolf asserts, the dramatist achieves this by contriving "an ending which is formal and comic, thus distancing Cain and exploding the scene in farce."[44] The closing image of Cain at his plow does offer the kind of comic explosion Woolf speaks of, for he continues to curse his servant, threatening to "hang the apon this plo, / with this rope, lo, lad, lo!" (459-60). But in its obvious recalling of the first scene of the play, in its several references to the devil and to the curse of Cain, and in its address to the spectators as Cain's "felows all" (462), this closing recalls the similarities of Cain and the members of the audience and reminds them of the fate of those who test their own logic against divine authority.

Noah and His Wife

The plays that present Noah and the flood continue the theme of divine authority that is prominent in earlier Old Testament scenes, but here the focus of the question shifts away from testing that power. Instead the playwrights seek to demonstrate the human response to divine control and the system it imposes. Especially after the intensity of the Cain and Abel plays, this movement to the domestic level--the troubles between Noah and his wife--must have been a welcome relief to the audience.

In terms of staging possibilities alone, both the textual evidence and the records about the plays indicate that the Noah story in the cycles was spectacular and popular--so much so that Chaucer relied on it as an important background in The Miller's Tale. When one considers the active involvement of the guilds in the creation of stage properties and scenery--perhaps even competing against one another for the most elaborate staging--it is logical to conclude that physically impressive dramatization became an essential component of this play.[45] Details about the ark itself, the mechanics of a stage flood, and the treatment of animals in the plays are not outlined clearly in stage directions, but several critics have examined the suggestions of staging in the plays to reach some important conclusions. Of primary interest is the idea that all the evidence seems to suggest stationary staging of the Noah play, at least at Wakefield.[46] The ludicrous image of God on the roof of a pageant wagon sending a messenger to Noah, a few feet away, is dispelled by such a theory and offers the dramatist more creative possibility than trying to usher an ark through crowded, narrow streets. The dramatic impact of the flood is also intensified through stationary staging, and at least in Towneley the textual evidence suggests that real water was an important stage setting for several plays.[47] The stylized presentation of the flood by waving a painted cloth, which may have been the technique at York, is thus dismissed in considerations of the Towneley play.

Similar attention to detail is evident in the playwrights' use of animals in the play. Several critics suggest that in the York and Chester plays the dialogue as Noah releases the dove leads one to believe that a bird was actually being released.[48] And M.D. Anderson remarks that "although the stage directions of the Chester Plays say that on the boards round the ark 'all the beasts and fowls must be painted' . . . a more realistic embarkation scene" is shown in so many examples of medieval art that live animals may have been used as well,[49] surely to the advantage of the dramatist who sought to involve the audience.

The spectators' interest in the Noah plays extends far beyond these physical devices, however, for the texts themselves are much more than flimsy vehicles for elaborate stage properties. The plays about Noah offer strong dramatic possibilities in themselves, for they have at their centers the sharp conflict that constitutes good drama. Unlike the earlier plays, here that contrast--particularly the struggle between Noah and his wife--is exploded comically on stage, inviting the audience to make active choices about the characters and situations being presented. This comedy is so involving, and so delightful, that losing sight of the larger conflicts in the plan of order is easy, in spite of the many references to it. Spectators are urged, through this combined influence of impressive staging and lively dramatization, to put themselves in the position of many of the characters in these plays: so engrossed in the activity and pleasures of this world that they do not see in the ark, the animals, and the flood a reminder of the permanence of divine order and the obligation of men to accept it.

The opening speeches of each of the cycle plays and the Newcastle fragment of Noah's ark move quickly to reiterate the conditions of man's Creation, his subsequent wickedness, and his disregard for his responsibility to God and other men. In most of the plays, it is God who makes this first declaration, as in the Cursor Mundi where this sinister backdrop is sketched:

> Al þis world bitrayeþ me
> þei han lafte me & my lawe
> Of me stonden þei noon awe
> Al is for eten þat fraunchise
> þat I ȝaf mon in paradise
> þe erþe wiþ synne is foul shent
> Al ri twisnes awey is went
> Foule lustes & wicked-hede
> Han filed þis world in lengþe & brede.[50]

Although the passage is tinged with a sense of pathos, with God as a tragic victim of man's sin, this initial characterization is used only as a prerequisite for inductive reasoning. If, as this passage indicates, men have ignored the conditions that have been set for them, then their bitter punishment is just, and God is characterized as distant and rational, not the "lord and lover" that one critic asserts him to be.[51] As God speaks in the economical opening of the Newcastle play, the logical structure serves to move the central action as quickly as possible:

```
Me rewes this world that I have wrought;
    No marvel if I do sae.
Their folk in earth I made of nought;
    Now are they fully my fae.
Vengeance now will I tae
    Of them that have grieved me ill.
Great floods shall over them gae,
    And run over hoope and hill.[52]
```

Here the playwright moves rapidly to a direct statement of God's intended punishment, using carefully structured end rhymes to link the cause with the dreaded effect. In York, this logical development spans more than three stanzas and begins with a detailed narration of Creation. It closes with emphasis on the equal strength God has in destruction:

```
    Bot sen they make me to repente
My werke I wroght so wele and trewe,
Wyth-owtyn seys will noght assente,
Bot euer is bowne more bale to brewe.
Bot for ther synnes þai shall be shente,
And for-done hoyly, hyde and hewe.
Of þam shall no more be mente,
Bot wirke þis werke I will al newe.
    Al newe I will þis worlde be wroght,
And waste away þat wonnys þer-in,
A flowyd a-bove þame shall be broght,
To stroye medilerthe, both more and myn.
                                (17-28)
```

Although the audience already knows God's reasons for destroying the earth, the Noah plays open with this reminder for several reasons. First, these speeches pull into focus the theme that persists in these Old Testament plays: divine authority and

70

human response to it. Second, and more important, they provide the context for the underlying conflict in the plays: the disparity between God's expectations and human ability to meet them.

The sources of this conflict differ among the cycles, but each play stresses a failure on man's part to comply with the will of God. In the Newcastle play God offers only a general comment that people "have grieved me ill" (6), and in Chester the audience is told simply that ". . . my people in deede and thought / are sett fowle in sinne" (3-4); the opening prayers of the N-Town and Towneley versions offer the greatest insight into the nature and extent of human disobedience. The playwrights' decision to allow criticism of sinners to be heard from earth before God asserts himself is a skillful choice. These lines by Noah in the N-Town version give the sense of a good man struggling to keep out of the evil that surrounds him:

> Ther may no man go þer owte
> but synne regnyth in every rowte
> In every place rownde a-bowte
> Cursydnes doth sprynge and sprede
>
> (23-26)

In the Wakefield version, this speech is much more impassioned, for after a long, emotional recounting of the details and conditions of Creation, Noah turns his attention to man. The tone of the Wakefield Noah reveals his absolute faith in the mercy and power of God, a faith which gives him enough sense to be concerned and frightened about the vengeance that God owes man:

> Bot now before his sight / euery liffyng leyde,
> Most party day and nyght / syn in word and dede
> ffull bold;
> Som in pride, Ire, and enuy,

Som in Couet[yse] & glotyny,
Som in sloth and lechery,
    And other wise many fold.

                            (48-54)

The criticism of sinners here is unique in its detail, but it
shares with the other cycles a similar introductory function.
Unlike the Chester dramatization, in which God ascribes virtue
to Noah by calling him "that righteous man" (18), here the
dramatist allows Noah to speak for himself and reveal his true
nature. Just as his criticism for earth is harsh, his praise
for God and his creation is sincere and joyous:

Myghtfull god veray / Maker of all that is,
Thre persons withoutten nay / oone god in endles
    blis,
Thou maide both nyght & day / beest, fowle, &
    fysh,
All creatures that lif may / wroght thou at thi
    wish,
    As thou wel myght;
The son, the moyne, verament,
Thou maide; the firmament,
The sternes also full feruent,
    To shyne thou maide ful bright.

                            (1-9)

In all of the cycles, this introductory material presents seriously the conditions that necessitate the flood. It also establishes a serious and complex context in which the simplest
domestic comedy can occur. Without the frame, the scenes depicting Noah and his wife would be only comic relief wedged
between the tragic stories of Cain-Abel and Abraham-Isaac.
Because all of the cycles make use of such frames of devout
prayers and divine proclamations, evidence points to a function
beyond comic relief. It seems clear that once again the audience was intended to be diverted temporarily from the meaning of

the play by the attractiveness of the lively middle scenes. The consistent appeals to popular traditions in the Middle Ages as the source of humor indicate the ease with which the audience would have responded. Here there is less shocking humor--like Cain's audacious cursing--than dramatized variations on familiar medieval jokes. The effect, however, remains the same as in the earlier plays: spectators are lured through the comedy to participate emotionally in the stage action.

One of the most obvious comic developments in the plays is based on Noah's age. Except for the Chester version, all of the plays contain direct statements by Noah about his age, usually as he ponders the immense task of building an ark. These descriptions of age follow the biblical references; nevertheless, emphasis on the feebleness that accompanies old age is used in several of the mystery cycles, even in the otherwise humorless N-Town play:

> How xuld I haue wytt a shypp for to make
> I am of ryght grett Age V.C. ȝere olde
> it is not for me þis werk to vndyr-take
> Ffor ffeynnesse of Age my leggys gyn ffolde.
>> (N-Town, 126-29)

> A! worthy lorde, wolde þou take heede,
> I am full olde and oute of qwarte,
> Pat me liste do no daies dede,
> Bot yf gret mystir me garte.
>> (York, 49-52)

> I am a man no worth at need,
>> For I am six hundred winters of eld.
> Unlusty I am to do such a deed,
>> Workhlooms for to work and weeld.
>>> (Newcastle, 77-80)

While each of these examples reveals the humility of Noah as he is faced with the responsibility of perpetuating life on earth, the discernible whining tone of the speaker undermines his virtue and places the negative image of the old man at the center of the action.[53] References in the Newcastle play to the fact that Noah is sleeping confirm such a view.

The most poetic of these passages, in the Towneley _Processus Noe_, is described by one critic as "a lyric _planctus_ of an old man."[54] Its comic tone, however, is evident in these lines:

> Sex hundreth yeris & od / haue I, without
> distance,
> In erth, as any sod / liffyd with grete grevance
> All way;
> And now I wax old,
> seke, sory, and cold,
> As muk apon mold
> I widder away.
>
> (57-63)

In all of the plays many such opportunities exist as skeletons for skilled actors to fill out in all their comic proportions. The withered man who, in the Towneley and York cycles, is bewildered at God's unusual request is a portrait of comic irony, for the audience, knowing the whole situation, laughs heartily at Noah's confusion.

In addition to its heightening of interest in the plays, this comic characterization is a useful vehicle for introducing several themes of the play. One of these is the trust Noah places in God. Because he is so feeble, Noah must rely on divine assistance to complete his task. The Chester play, stressing Noah's role as "servante" (17, 326), makes this dependence relentlessly simple, for he accepts the assignment with gladness and works diligently and contentedly until the ark is complete. His attitude is summarized in his statement, "Lord, at your byddinge I am bayne" (145). The N-Town Noah also overcomes his initial reluctance with remarkable ease. After the angel who presents God's orders explains that "God xal enforme þe and rewle þe ful ryght" (131), Noah responds with an eagerness to serve: "I am ful redy as god doth me bydde" (134).

The York play expands this theme by demonstrating the rejuvenation that Noah undergoes as a result of God's grace. As in other plays, Noah's inexperience with ship-building leads to a narration of the specific dimensions and features of the ark. In the York Shipwrights' play, a burst of energy immediately motivates the old man, a comic contrast to the description of his frailty:

> A! blistfull lord, þat al may beylde,
> I thanke þe hartely both euer and ay,
> Fyfe hundreth wyntres I am of elde,
> Me thynk þer ʒeris as yestirday.
> Ful wayke I was and all vn-welde,
> My werynes is wente away,
> To wyrk þis werke here in þis feylde
> Al be my-selfe I will assaye.
>
> (89-96)

Such a conversion is necessary in that play if Noah is to find the joy and energy in construction that the next lines suggest. When he begins to grow weary, reminding the spectators that "slyke trauayle for to be bente, / Is harde to hym þat is þus olde" (116-17), the value of relying on the strength of God is once again stressed: God comforts Noah by stating that "þis werke is nere an ende" (120) and that "I sall þe socoure for certayne, / Tille alle þe care awey be kaste" (142-43).

The Newcastle presentation offers a concise statement of

the trust Noah places in God. Accepting the fact that God's will shall be fulfilled, Noah explains the only conditions for completing the ark:

> For I was never in my life
> Of kind or craft to burthen a boat;
> For I have neither ruff nor ryff,
> Spyer, sprund, sprout, not sprot.
> Christ be the shaper of this ship,
> For a ship need make I mot
>
> (81-86)

The comic enumeration of the skills and tools that Noah does not possess, as well as his anachronistic reference to Christ, offers the audience a chance to laugh at his ineptitude. The difference between this Noah and others is that here he immediately lets the spectators know that he understands what he is doing:

> Therefore, men, or ever you blin,
> You mend your life and turn your thought,
> For of my work I will begin.
> So well were me were all forth brought.
>
> (91-94)

His faith gives him the security to turn his thought away from the comic implications of building an enormous ark on dry land and toward the fact that God has selected him for this important work.

Comic characterization of Noah also incorporates antifeminist tradition. The weakness of an old man calls up in the minds of the medieval spectators images of the henpecked or cuckolded husband, and in the Corpus Christi drama this association is the primary source of humor. Noah's wife, mentioned only briefly in the Genesis account as part of the assemblage to board the ark, is developed fully in all of the cycles except the N-Town. Her presence and her interaction with Noah add another dimension to the plays, for without an examination of Noah's earthly relationships--what one critic calls "the very stuff of drama"[55]--these plays might consist of only loosely connected spectacles and prayers. The rounding out of Noah's wife gives energy and focus to the plays as it develops an important theme in the Old Testament presentations: maistry in its earthly and spiritual connotations.

Although an early study credits the medieval playwrights with the characterization of Noah's wife as a termagant,[56] evidence in literature, art, and folklore suggests that a composite sketch was formed through medieval legend.[57] Specific association of Noah's wife with recalcitrance is persistent in heretical sects, where, for example, the Gnostic Book of Noria is reputed to portray her "desire to thwart her husband in his heaven-sent mission through setting fire to the Ark repeatedly. . . ."[58] Mill similarly dispels the notion that the Newcastle playwright was ingenious to involve the devil in the disobedience of Noah's wife. Instead, this and other cycle plays grew out of a tradition that established Noah's wife as a stubborn shrew at odds with her husband.

The Newcastle fragment also employs many other legends about the wife of Noah that Mill outlines. Much as in the scene with Eve, the devil tempts Noah's wife to work against him. Traditional alliances between them are stated directly as the devil approaches her:

> To Noah's wife will I wynd,
>   Gare her believe in me;

                                  In faith she is my friend,
                                       She is both whunt and slee.

                                  Rest well, rest well, my own dere dame!
                                  UXOR NOAH DICAT. Welcome, bewschere; what is thy
                                       name?
                                                                        (109-14)

Unlike the other cycle presentations, the Newcastle fragment
does not portray the flood. Instead, the triumph of Noah over
the satanic plot to thwart his building becomes the climax of
the play. Realizing that the situation is out of his hands when
his wife cannot discern "whether thou be friend or foe" (183),
Noah seeks divine intervention:

                                  God send me help in hy
                                       To clink yon nails twain;
                                  God send me help in hy
                                       Your hand to hold again.
                                  That all well done may be
                                       My strokes not be in vain.
                                                                        (186-91)

His abiding hope and trust in God sustain Noah, resulting in
both earthly reconciliation and spiritual redemption. The devil
remains the villain throughout, cursing the audience as he exits
the stage and closes the play: "I pray to Dolphin, prince of
dead, / Scald you all in his lead, / That never a one of you
thrive nor thee" (204-06).

The Newcastle audience would have recognized several other
features of the Noah's wife legends, particularly devil-naming
and use of an intoxicating potion. Mill cites these features as
characteristic of the popular legends, in which Noah's wife
becomes responsible for bringing the devil on board the ark.[59]
The devil presents Noah's wife with a potion "that is made of a
mightful main" (133), strong enough to poison Noah. Knowing

what was next, the audience enjoyed the trap that Noah sets for himself by remarking on his age and weariness. In the guise of a comforting nurse, the villainous wife deceives her husband:

> Sit down here beside me,
>   Thou hast full weary baynes.
> Have eaten, Noah, as might I thee,
> And soon a drink I shall give thee,
>   Such drank thou never ayns.
>
> (151-55)

The dramatic irony is comic here, for the spectators know that somehow Noah will overcome this obstacle and save men and beasts from the flood. And in this satanic creature, they are reminded of the beguiling shrews whom they have met in popular literature and in real life.

The devil-naming incident follows, although more in implication than in repetition of the legend. Mill summarizes this aspect of the tale by citing a Wogul folk-tale:

> The old man says: Come on board! She does not move. Again he says: Come on board! She does not. For the third time he calls: Come on board, you devil. Then Xul'ater [the spirit of darkness] creeps into the wife's belly and gets into the ship. At the end of the conflagration he springs out alive.[60]

No such timing or subtlety is evident in the Newcastle fragment: immediately after he drinks the potion, Noah shouts as if mad, "What the devil!" (156). In spite of this semblance to the folk-tale narration, the devil's plan to sneak aboard the ark does not succeed here, for the curse of his wife--"The devil of hell thee take" (184)--is negated by the unending hope of Noah.

Another important resource for the playwrights is the extensive antifeminist tradition, which emerges in much of medieval literature.[61] In general, Christian theory of the period supports the contention that women, as a sex, are not only inferior to men but are evil as well. This excerpt from Tertullian offers such a view:

> And do you not know that you are Eve? God's sentence hangs still over all your sex and His punishment weighs down upon you. You are the devil's gateway; you are she who first violated the forbidden tree and broke the law of God. It was you who coaxed your way around him whom the devil had not the force to attack. With what ease you shattered that image of God: man! Because of the death you merited, the Son of God had to die.[62]

In the popular tradition, attention is often directed at the effect this corrupt sex has on men. Emphasis on the wily nature of women and their malicious cores, despite deceptively pleasing exteriors, is a prevalent theme. The <u>Proverbs of Alfred</u>, which offer concise bits of advice, caution readers against these treacheries:

> Ne wurþ þu neuer so wod.
> ne so wyn-drunke.
> þat euere segge þine wife.
> alle þine wille.
> For if þu iseye þe bi-vore.
> þine i-vo alle.
> And þu hi myd worde
> iwreþþed heuedest.
> Ne scholde heo hit lete.
> for þing lyuyinde.
> þat heo ne scholde þe forþ vp-breyde.
> of þine baleu-syþes.
>
>   .   .   .
>
> Many appel is bryht wiþ-vte.
> and Bitter wiþ-inne.
> So is mony wymmon.
>
>   .   .   .
>
> wymmon wepeþ for mod.
> oftere þan for eny god.

80

> And ofte lude and stille,
> for to vordrye hire wille.
> Heo wepeþ oþer-hwile.
> for to do þe gyle.[63]

Ballads and folk traditions echo these sentiments in a more amusing style, which often mocks the women and sides with their helpless husbands. An example is a humorous ballad which shows the lack of choices offered to men when they are confronted with belligerent wives:

> How say ye, women þat husbondis haue?
> Will not ye ther honowr saue,
> & call them 'lowsy stynkyng knave'?
>   In villa!
>
>   . . .
>
> Ye, husbondis all, with on asent,
> Lett your wyffys haue þer yntent,
> Or suerly ye will be shent
>   In villa.
> Ytt ys hard a-yenst þe strem to stryve,
> For hym þat cast hym for to thryve,
> He mvst aske leve of hys wyff,
>   In villa.
> of ellis by God & by the rode,
> Be he never so wyld & wode,
> Hys here shall grow thorow his hode
>   In villa.[64]

The ability of women to achieve such power, in spite of the fact that civil and Christian law renders them inferior, is a source of amazement for the speaker here and source of humor for his audience.

Cycle playwrights, except for the N-Town writer, play with this idea of feminine power as they dramatize the shrewish character of Noah's wife. Like the ballad writers, the dramatists focus on this power as an inhibiting force, one that in this case prevents Noah from complying with divine command. As in the ballads, the focus here is on the comic effects of this power, on the men who are subverted by it. When his wife refuses to board the ark, the Chester Noah echoes the spirit of the ballad, for he relinquishes his _maistry_ for the sake of expediency:

> Lord, that weomen bine crabbed aye,
> and non are meeke, I dare well saye.
> That is well seene by mee todaye
> In witnesse of you eychone.
> Good wiffe, lett be all this beare
> that thou makest in this place here,
> for all the weene that thou arte mastere--
> and soe thou arte, by sayncte John.
>
> (105-12)

His tone, at once sarcastic and patronizing, appeals to a common woe among members of the audience who have found themselves in similar predicaments with their spouses. This direct emotional involvement with the audience is possible when the dramatists weave familiar tradition and legend into the biblical narrative of the Noah story, and the characterization of Noah's wife in light of this background is bait that most of the playwrights could not ignore.

When commanded by her husband to leap into the completed ark, Noah's wife in the Chester version seems to undergo a vivid metamorphosis. In the economical construction pageant at the opening of that play, Noah's wife stresses the weakness and docility of women, as she and her daughters-in-law work cooperatively with the men:

> And wee shall bringe tymber to,
> for wee mon nothinge ells doe--
> women bynne weake to underfoe
> any great travell.
>
> (65-68)

The words and actions of the other characters confirm her stereotypical view: the men bring tools, and the women bring light wood, sludge, hay, and chips for a cooking fire. Knowledge of the legends and traditions associated with Noah's wife immediately adds a tongue-in-cheek quality to the recitations of the women, for the passage becomes as obvious in its humor as these lines from an antifeminist ballad:

> The stedfastnes of women will neuer be don,
> So Jentyll, so curtes they be euery chon,
> Meke as a lambe, still as a stone,
> Croked nor Crabbed ffynd ye none!
>   Cuius contrarium verum est.
> Men be more Cumbers a thowsand fold,
> & I mervayll how they dare be so bold,
> Agaynst women for to hold,
> Seyng them so pascyent! softe & cold.
>   Cuius contrarium verum est.[65]

Thus the innocuous remark by Noah's wife prepares the spectators for the scene which they anticipate, the scene in which the helpful, obedient wife will reveal her true nature.

Although in this cycle the development of Noah's wife is not as extensive as in the York and Towneley presentations, this characterization reminds the audience of the theme that runs consistently beneath the surface of the play: the harmony which is possible through acceptance of the divine plan. It is not coincidental that the first sign of rebellion appears after Noah's rapid construction of the ark. All of his mission has progressed smoothly, and one can imagine that the staging of this scene was more an unfolding or simple linking of prefabricated parts than a belabored construction:

> With topcastle and bowespreete,
> bothe cordes and roopes I have all meete
> to sayle forthe at the nexte weete--

this shippe is at an ende.

(93-96)

His satisfaction in finishing the task is undermined in the minds of the spectators by the difficulty that they know awaits him. However cruel this laughter may be, the audience enjoys the dramatic irony of seeing Noah set himself up for a greater challenge than he has faced. The retort given by his wife would have provided an opportunity for comic expansion, as the audience delights in witnessing the shock that they have already imagined:

> In fayth, Noe, I had as leeve thou slepte
> For all thy Frenyshe fare,
> I will not doe after thy reade.

(99-101)

In the lines that develop this domestic conflict, Noah and his wife are fixed in the roles that the popular tradition has cast them: henpecked husband and shrew.

A unique feature of the Chester play is its interruption of this quarrel with a detailed speech by God. In all other versions, the plans for the ark are pronounced at the onset; the Chester playwright, however, intensifies dramatic and thematic effect by inserting here God's directive for loading the ark with animals and provisions. Dramatically, this intrusion on the enjoyable domestic scene, in which the Old Testament figure for Christ is reduced to a sighing, impotent old man, serves to heighten the involvement of the spectators. In God's rehearsal of what is already very familiar to them--the kind of animals, "twayne and noe more" (125)--the members of the audience find time to let their imaginations wander. With pleasure they anticipate the full-scale argument that they know is coming, and the context of the ark and the flood are minimized in this intense expectation of unsophisticated comedy.

On a thematic level, this speech by God is also important, for embedded in his words are several important reminders of the theme of divine authority that has echoed through the Old Testament plays. The correct relationship between the corresponding parts of the great chain of being are stressed in repetition of the simple parallelisms suggested by the biblical narrative. Much emphasis is given to the male/female relationship: "hee and shee, make to make" (119), "male and female" (122) and "the hee and shee together" (124). In contrast to the simple references in N-Town, "Of euery kyndys best a cowpyl þou take" (120), and in York, "Of ilka kynde þou sall take twoo, / Bothe male and femalle fare in fere" (130-31), the Chester dramatization deliberately points to those relationships that weaken God's plan for order when they are unharmonious.

The dramatic effect is stronger than the thematic in this case, for even with such simple and obvious reminders, secular comedy dominates the religious story. Whereas the other cycles show Noah's wife resisting entrance into the ark for odd, trivial reasons, such as having "tolis to trusse" (York, 110), the Chester play is unique in its emphasis on a clearly secular--and medieval--reason for hesitation: her devotion to her gossips. At first her intentions seem charitable and Christian, as she herself indicates:

> But I have my gossips, everyechone,
> one foote further I will not gone.

They shall not drowne, by sayncte John,
and I may save there life.

The loved me full well, by Christe.
But thou wilte lett them into thy chiste,
elles rowe forthe, Noe, when thy liste
and gett thee a newe wyfe.

(201-08)

This faithfulness to one's friends appears noble, especially when Noah's wife--carried away by her own moving speech--dramatically threatens him with an ultimatum. Even in this tragic reminder that many lives were lost in the flood, the Chester dramatist invites a comic response: there is no possibility of a new wife when all of humanity is about to be destroyed. His response that "such another I doe not knowe" (210) reinforces this reaction to her threat.

Another careful addition is the Chester playwright's choice to have the gossips speak for themselves--unlike the situation in the York play, where Noah's wife laments that her friends "are ouere flowen with floode" (152). One sees in their song exactly the kind of cameraderie that these women offer one another:

And lett us drinke or wee departe,
for oftetymes wee have done soe.
For at one draught thou drinke a quarte,
and soe will I doe or I goe.

Here is a pottell full of malnesaye good and
stronge;
yt will rejoyse both harte and tonge.
Though Noe thinke us never soe longe,
yett wee wyll drinke atyte.

(229-36)

They drink in the face of disaster, not out of a sense of despair, loss, or even escape, but rather for the sheer pleasure intoxication brings. The comic development prevents the spectators from mourning the sinners, and instead shows the gossips to be similar to the people one might meet in an ale-house. The tone and implication of the gossips' song was also well known through tradition, for a popular ballad echoes these voices:

> "How say ye, gossippis? Is þis wyn good?"
> "Pat is it," quod Elynore, "by þe rode!
> It chereth þe hart & comforteth þe blod.
>   Such jonkers amonge
>   Shall make vs leve long.
>   Good gossippis myn, a!"[66]

The fact that these women comfort one another because of their domineering husbands strikes another interesting parallel between the ballad and Chester play. This particularly harsh presentation of women reveals the motives of Noah's wife, reducing her reluctance from magnanimity to petty selfishness. The lack of vision on the part of the gossips in the ballad is also repeated in the play: as Elynore is blind to the obvious comparison of the "Muscadell" to sacrificial wine, the Chester gossips are myopic in their rejoicing at the brink of destruction. Here, however, as elsewhere in the play, the Chester dramatist strives for a comic control of the scene. Lively contest, therefore, moves the first part of the play forward and the religious theme to the surface.

None of the Middle English Noah plays, however, synchronizes the comic and religious forces as carefully or as effectively as the Towneley _Processus Noe_, a play recognized as "the work of a genius,"[67] even by critics who are dumbfounded by its humor. Here, the comic characterizations of Noah and his wife are brought to their full dramatic potential. The wrangling between them, on the surface similar to conflicts in the York cycle, is more sophisticated than the other presentations, for here the themes in the quarrel--shouted angrily or mumbled in asides to the audience--add a new perspective to the religious ideals of the play by "obscuring the allegorical significance of . . . Christ summoning the sinner into the church."[68] Critical assessments that find evidence for a parallel between secular and religious scenes in the play[69] miss the intense dramatic mechanisms by which such a realization works in the minds of the spectators. The Wakefield Master hammers together elements from folklore, antifeminist tradition, and contemporary culture to construct a solid statement on the nature of divine order and authority. What makes the play so effective dramatically is that the audience enjoys each comic blow of the hammer--its noise, its frantic action, its power--without realizing the monument that is being constructed until the last piece is in place.

The contrast between heavenly and earthly systems of order, a repeated theme for the Wakefield Master,[70] is stressed several times in Noah's opening prayer and in God's response, especially in their reiteration of the elevated position God maintains. Noah proves in his humble prayer, in his reference to himself as "a symple knafe" (173), that he understands and accepts the conditions God has established for him:

> _Deus_. Syn I haue maide all thyng / that is
>   liffand,
> Duke, emperour, and kyng / with myne awne hand,
> ffor to haue thare likyng / bi see & bi sand,

88

```
      Euery man to my bydyng / shuld be bowand
            ffull feruent;
      That maide man sich a creatoure,
      ffarest of favoure,
      Man must luf me paramoure,
            by reson, and repent.
```
                                                    (73-81)

As soon as this simple condition is reduced to its human level,
it grows in complexity and becomes much more difficult to accept.   If Noah does love God above all, then he must build an
ark on dry land against all human reason.   Noah's response
indicates his ambivalence toward God's request, for while his
seeking a blessing reveals his willingness to God, "the better
may we stere / the ship that we shall hafe" (175), his shift of
attention toward his wife's reaction weakens the image of him as
a man confident in his devotion:

```
      lord, homward will I hast / as fast as that I
            may;
      my [wife] will I frast / what she will say,
            [Exit Deus.]
      And I am agast / that we get som fray
            Betwixt vs both;
      ffor she is full tethee,
      ffor litill oft angre,
      If any thyng wrang be,
            Soyne is she wroth.
```
                                                    (182-89)

Fear of God is easily transformed to fear of his wife, and this
unique preparation for her appearance on stage hints to the
Towneley spectators that the husband/wife relationship is not
characterized by harmony.   The insults with which Noah is immediately bombarded confirm this impression, as Noah's wife proves
herself to be the termagant of legend:

```
      Now, as euer myght I thryfe / the wars I thee
            see;
      Do tell me belife / where has thou thus long be?
      To dede may we dryfe / or lif for the,
```

ffor want.
When we swete or swynk,
thou dos what thou thynk,
Yit of mete and of drynk
haue we veray skant.

(191-98)

Her criticism of her husband's activity is a contemporary characteristic, for she measures the worth of an activity by the
practical benefits she reaps from it.

Her faith in God is also ruled by such pragmatism: in the
ensuing argument, for example, she solicits God and Mary several
times as a means of reinforcing her complaints about husbands in
general--and her husband in particular. She even requests that
God make Noah as miserable as he claims to be: "ffrom euen vnto
morow, / Thou spekis euer of sorow; / God send the onys thi
fill!" (205-07). Such a statement works on several different
levels. The irony is that the audience knows that God has,
indeed, planned quite a bit of sorrow for the world and that--
for once, at least--Noah's fear is justified. The comic irony
in this statement is that Noah's wife reveals her convenient
belief in God's authority, one that is directly opposed to the
meek, constant faith of her husband.

The resulting conflict is reminiscent of the marital quar-
rels one is likely to encounter in popular medieval literature,
with a small dispute brought to blows because of generaliza-
tions, accusations, and threats.[71] What is unique here is that
Noah responds to the taunts of his wife much more brutally than
in the other cycles, behaving more like the frustrated bully in
the ballads than the weary, but patient, soul-mate one sees, for

example, in the Chester. Carey stresses that this transition is especially evident when contrasted with the particularly pious image of Noah in the opening of the play: "Gone is his dignity, his patriarchal prestige, which made him able to talk with God on almost equal footing."[72] After his wife's explanation that at times she "shall smyte and smyle, / And qwite hym his mede" (215-16), Noah reacts with unrestrained anger: "We! hold thi tong, ram-skyt / or I shall the still" (217). His indignation is entirely personal--certainly not the righteous anger of medieval Christian theory that is intended to nudge the wife toward a mending of her ways.[73] He strikes her readily, declaring, "Apon the bone shal it byte" (220); when she hits him back, he claims that it is his right to beat her.

The playwright is obviously working on a secular level here, for the couple on stage seem--in their references to clothing and in the medieval name, Gill, ascribed to Noah's wife--to be a pair the spectators know, not the allegorical figure of Christ and his obedient spouse, as suggested by patristic critics. The basis of their dispute is also secular, with repeated emphasis on debt and repayment. What prevents this comic development from taking over the play as it does in York is the Wakefield Master's sense of timing. When the argument reaches its climax, the playwright quickly drops the bottom out of the comedy by delaying the resolution and returning the participants to their proper roles. Noah offers only this brief and inadequate explanation for his giving up the fight:

> Thou can both byte and whyne,
> with a rerd;

ffor all if she stryke,
yit fast will she skryke,
In fayth I hold none slyke
    In all medill-erd;

Bot I will kepe charyte / ffor I haue at do.
                        (229-35)

The development that follows, their separation so that Noah can build the ark, is necessary for the sake of the narrative and the dramatic spectacle: at some point an ark must appear. The dramatist's choice to place this construction in the midst of a banal dispute pushes the impact of that scene beyond the level of visual spectacle. The spectators are asked to continue viewing the play at the same level of intensity, for they seek to discover in this scene indications of the argument that was left unfinished. Comic possibilities which are evident in the text assure that characterization remain constant: Noah channels his frustration toward Gill into energy in suiting the ark to God's precise commands, and his wife involves herself in spinning, presumably off stage. Noah, emphasizing his age and decrepitness, struggles with his back and his "bonys" (253, 268) almost as much as he had squabbled with his wife. And all the while he is making "the top and the sayll . . . the helme and the castell" (271-72), the audience is waiting for the human struggle that they know will resume.

Once again, the timing is critical, for Noah's praise of God and confidence in his plan is immediately threatened when his wife confronts him. Her reason for defiance is unique to this cycle, for here Gill is rebellious not because of the devil or a simple inclination to be stubborn. She reacts with a realistic human emotion: "I dase and I dedir / ffor ferd of that tayll" (314-15). The playwright uses this realism to a dramatic advantage, for from this stance Noah's wife can challenge the idea of divine authority and order. The obedience of the sons is comically contrasted with her fearful hesitation, and the spectators come to anticipate the contumacy that they know is inevitable:

> <u>Noe</u>. Be not aferd, haue done / trus sam oure
>   gere,
> That we be ther or none / without more dere.
>   <u>primus filius</u>. It shall be done full sone /
>   brether, help to bere.
>   <u>Secundus filius</u>. ffull long shall I not
>   hoyne / to do my devere,
>   Brether sam.
> <u>Tercius filius</u>. without any yelp,
> At my myght shall I help.
>   <u>Vxor</u>. Yit for drede of a skelp
>   help well thi dam.
>   (316-24)

Comic building, slow here, increases in velocity as water begins to circle the hill upon which Noah's wife sits and spins. Her fear is thinly disguised in such remarks as "Yit reede I no man let me, / ffor drede of a knok" (341-42), and "Yei, noe, go cloute thi shone / the better will thai last" (353). While she remarks to her daughters-in-law that "All in vayn ye carp" (360), her growing sense of urgency reveals the uneasiness she feels as she finds that Noah has been telling the truth. V.A. Kolve suggests that a "domestic storm" brews with the same intensity and for the same reason as the flood itself, for Noah's correct interpretations of the threatening sky (343-52) become a metaphoric way of discussing the marital dispute:

> The seven planets have left their places in the
> sky; all is chaos and lack of order. . . . And

to this macrocosmic anarchy the drama relates
the microcosm.   God's great world is turned
upside down just as is man's little world, and
for the same reason: proper maistrye has been
destroyed.[74]

The theory that actual water was used in the staging of this play offers a vivid explanation for Gill's sudden decision to board the ark. Even more important, however, is that for once Noah has left the choice in her hands:

<u>Noe</u>. Peter! I traw we dote;
without any more note
    Come in if ye will.

<u>Vxor</u>. Yei, water nyghys so nere / that I sit
        not dry,
Into ship with a byr / therfor will I hy
ffor drede that I drone here.

                                        (367-72)

Unlike the N-Town play (which presents complete obedience throughout the play), the Chester play (which offers a sudden, unexplained change in Noah's wife), or the York play (which shows Noah's wife being carried aboard the ark), the Towneley version portrays the resolution to board the ship with careful attention to dramatic effect. The Towneley character has too much conviction to be coerced so easily. Also, her challenge to authority--earthly and divine--has been so convincing that the dramatist is faced with a difficult religious problem: he must resolve the spectators' question of authority as he presents her yielding. This is accomplished entirely through comic emotional release in the final confrontation between husband and wife.

As she reaches the door of the ark, Noah's wife digs in her heels once more, declaring "I will not for thi bydyng, / go from doore to mydyng" (375-76). Setting aside his patience and his

94

obedience to the will of God, Noah retaliates with the threat of whipping her. Such remarks are simply bait for his wife, for they encourage her to resist even further. The flood, their watching sons, the mercy of God in saving them--these are all forgotten as they once again raise their fists and threaten one another. Here is one more opportunity to criticize the opposite sex, and neither takes the chance of missing it:

> Vxor. Lord, I were at ese / and hertely full
>   hoylle,
> Might I onys haue a measse / of wedows coyll;
> ffor this saull, without lese / shuld I dele
>   penny doyll,
> so wold me, no frese / that I se on this sole
>   of wifis that ar here,
> ffor the life that thay leyd,
> Wold thare husbandis were dede,
> ffor, as euer ete I brede,
>   So wold I oure syre were.
>
> Noe. Yee men that has wifis / whyls they ar
>   yong,
> If ye luf youre lifis / chastice thare tong:
> Me thynk my hert ryfis / both levyr and long,
> To se sich stryfis / wedmen emong;
>   Bot I,
> As haue I blus,
> shall chastyse this.

(388-403)

In their direct addresses to the audience and their pathetic appeals to universal woes of marriage, the actors who deliver these lines are assured of the spectators' intense involvement. The dilemma Noah's wife faces is a typical human response: she recognizes her need to board the ark but does not want to yield the power she senses in independence. It is an uncomfortable stance for the audience as well as for Gill: for all its comedy, as one critic explains, her resistance is "a serious reminder of the battle which we all face with the 'old man' in us [Ephesians iv.22-24]."[75] The physical comedy that erupts thus offers catharsis for both characters and spectators, as the exhaustion of rebellion takes its toll:

> Noe. . . . In this hast let vs ho,
> ffor my bak is nere in two.
> Vxor. And I am bet so blo
>   That I may not thryfe.

(411-14)

The reproach of their angry sons as the weary parents enter the ark reminds them—and also the audience—of their proper positions. Noah establishes control of the ship, in a physical as well as figurative sense, and his wife assumes the role of chief mate.

The symbol of the ark as a source of peace and protection could no more vividly be depicted than in the changed interaction between Noah and his wife:

> Noe. This is a grete flood / wife, take hede.
> Uxor. So me thoght, as I stode / we are in grete
>   drede.

(424-25)

Aboard the ark, they are transformed to the cooperative couple that epitomizes harmonious service to their creator. The struggles between them for control are completely relaxed.[76] Noah even gives his wife the helm as he sounds the depths, and he seeks her advice in choosing a bird to find some sign of hope.

This calm, yet emotionally stirring, conclusion to the play would be impossible were it not for the comic developments in the earlier scenes. The N-Town conclusion reads, like the rest of the play, as a prayer spoken in parts: "Ffor joye of þis token ryght hertyly we tende / oure lord god to worchep a songe lete vs synge" (252-53). The conclusion of the _Processus Noe_, however, is more like a dramatized prayer, for the sense of relief in the restoration of harmony and the joy in the family's acceptance of their positions as servants are brought to life through the seemingly unrelated brawls on stage. Compared to beating one another senseless and resisting divine authority at every opportunity, simple and joyful acceptance of one's position is shown in its most positive, appealing light.

Summary

In these cycle plays of the Old Testament, several common elements reveal a similarity in dramatic purpose. The position of humanity in middle-earth is stressed repeatedly, even suggested in what is known of the staging; and the extremes between which humans are pitted become dynamic opposing forces that the audience is never allowed to forget. The confusion that results from man's position is also developed consistently in these plays, as the central characters engage in external and internal struggles about the side they must choose.

In the best wrought of the Old Testament cycle plays, the dramatists use comedy to project this state of confusion onto the spectators, encouraging them to participate emotionally in the contumacy enacted before them. By comically rounding out and humanizing the traditionally evil characters, by endowing their arguments with vivid detail and logic, and by minimizing the dramatic impact of the Old Testament models of virtue, the playwrights cloud the established images of good and wicked.

Their involvement in lively--even coarse--comic scenes subtly pushes the members of the audience to an uneasy position, from which they would readily escape by immersing themselves in the antics on stage.

The emotional level, particularly in the plays by the Wakefield Master, builds to a comic plateau that may easily be shifted--at the same intensity--to something serious and calm. Just as the characters abruptly give in to the farce and fall into exhausted postures of devotion, the spectators, too, reach a point of emotional fatigue from which traditional religious responses once again seem logical and reassuring. As one critic notes, broad comedy is effective in achieving this effect: "it efficaciously purges the spirit of rebellion from the characters, and through them, from the spectators."[77]

Through comedy, the complacent audience is coaxed through a cycle of faith and doubt, ultimately strengthening their belief by playfully granting freedom to consider other choices. The cycle dramatists, particularly in Towneley and York, realize that the Old Testament virtues of obedience and subservience are not attractive when examined rationally or by earthly standards; their plays, therefore, use intense, shocking comedy not to divert the spectators but to bring about acceptance on an emotional level.[78] The questions of authority and response to it are thus resolved for the spectators, so that they approach the plays of the New Testament with a heightened awareness of their role in the divine plan.

Notes

[1] For general discussions of staging in the cycle plays, see these accounts: Glynne Wickham, *Early English Stages*, I: 1300-1576 (London: Routledge and Kegan Paul, 1966); William Tydeman, "Street Theatre," in *The Theatre of the Middle Ages* (London: Cambridge University Press, 1978), pp. 86-120; Martin Stevens, "The Staging of the Wakefield Plays," *Research Opportunities in Renaissance Drama*, 11 (1968), 115-28; Alan H. Nelson, "Some Configurations of Staging in Medieval English Drama," in *Middle English Drama*, Jerome Taylor and Alan H. Nelson, eds. (Chicago: The University of Chicago Press, 1972), pp. 116-47; and Margaret Dorrell, "Two Studies of the York Corpus Christi Play," *Leeds Studies in English*, N.S. 6 (1972), 63-111.

[2] "The Creation, and the Fall of Lucifer," in *York Plays*, ed. Lucy Toulmin Smith (1885; rpt. New York: Russell & Russell, 1963), ll. 1-4. Subsequent references to the York cycle shall make use of this edition, hereafter cited by line numbers in parentheses.

[3] "De Celi, Angelorom, et Infirne Speciun Creacion Pagina," in *The Chester Mystery Cycle*, I, ed. R.M. Lumiansky and David Mills (Early English Text Society, s.s. 3, London: Oxford University Press, 1974), ll. 3-4. Subsequent references to the Chester cycle shall be from this edition and cited by line numbers in parentheses.

[4] In York, at least, Peter Holding finds evidence in God's direct address to the sun and moon to suggest that a procession of Creation, "perhaps coupled with a tableau utilizing the guild's skill in plaster work," enhanced the act of Creation to make it "visually impressive." In "Stagecraft in the York Cycle," *Theatre Notebook*, 34 (1980), 54.

[5] "The Creation," in *The Towneley Plays*, ed. George England and Alfred W. Pollard (1897; rpt. Early English Text Society, e.s. 71, London: Oxford University Press, 1966), ll. 13-18. Subsequent references to the Towneley cycle shall be to this edition and cited by line numbers in parentheses.

[6] JoAnna Dutka asserts that the use of music in the plays as a means of reinforcing the stage action is strongly suggested in the Chester *Creation*, so that God's order would be symbolized in the harmonious liturgical music accompanying his entrances and exits: "the organ represents the house of God; bells, the expression of His word; and wind producing the sound of horns, the breath of life." In "Mysteries, Minstrels, and Music," *Comparative Drama*, 8 (1974), 116-17.

[7] Hanning, p. 28.

[8] Rosalie M. O'Connell classifies Lucifer with other "illegitimate royal figures," who use verbal parody "under the assumption that if they speak like God they will be able to act like Him. The tyrants realize that God's omnipotence is expressed through His dynamic word; this is the manifestation of the divine, and this is the power they covet and claim." In "Sovereignty through Speech in the Corpus Christi Mystery Plays," Renascence, 33 (1981), 118.

[9] Hanning, p. 29.

[10] Holding proposes that the visual effect of this boasting was achieved partly through stagecraft, for in York the same elaborate mechanism used to lower God from heaven may have been a vehicle for demonstrating Lucifer's imitation of God--"a wonderfully vivid representation of pride," p. 52.

[11] For a detailed explanation of the evidence for varied, but meaningful, presentations of hell in medieval drama and art, see Donald Clive Stuart, "The Stage Setting of Hell and the Iconography of the Middle Ages," The Romanic Review, 14 (1913), 330-42. Robert Hughes, in Heaven and Hell in Western Art (New York: Stein and Day Publishers, 1968), includes many vivid medieval examples from the pictorial tradition. See also John Marshall, who focuses on the spectacle of English representations of hell in "The Medieval English Stage: A Graffito of a Hell-Mouth Scaffold?" Theatre Notebook, 34 (1980), 101-02.

[12] Stevens, p. 123.

[13] An example is Louis H. Leiter's emphasis on type as "an important dramatic and aesthetic device" which "shows, however statically, the power, presence, and persuasion of God rolling through the drama." In "Typology, Paradigm, Metaphor, and Image in the York Creation of Adam and Eve," Drama Survey, 7 (1969), 113-32.

[14] This gradual alienation of man from God is emphasized by several critics as the most severe effect of moral and physical decline that occurs in Augustine's first age of the world. See, for example, James Dean, "The World Grown Old and Genesis in Middle English Historical Writings," Speculum, 57 (1982), 548-68; and Edith Hartnett, "Cain in the Medieval Towneley Play," Annuale Mediaevale, 12 (1971), 21-29.

[15] Anne Cooper Gay, "The 'Stage' and the Staging of the N-Town Plays," Research Opportunities in Renaissance Drama, 10 (1967), 138.

[16] For a survey of the traditions of Cain evident in literature and folklore, see Oliver F. Emerson, "Legends of Cain, Especially in Old and Middle English," PMLA, 21 (1906), 831-929.

[17] See, as examples of this approach to characterization, David Lyle Jeffrey, "Stewardship in the Wakefield Mactacio Abel and Noe Plays," American Benedictine Review, 22 (1971), 67-70; Clifford Davidson, "After the Fall: Design in the Old Testament Plays in the York Cycle," Mediaevalia, 1 (1975), 6; and Walter Meyers, A Figure Given: Typology in the Wakefield Plays (Pittsburgh: Duquesne University Press, 1970), pp. 50-52. See also D.W. Robertson, who shifts the focus from typology to tropology, an approach which "releases Scriptural events from the limits of space and time and makes them perennial." In "The Question of 'Typology' and the Wakefield Mactacio Abel," American Benedictine Review, 25 (1974), 160.

[18] John Gardner, The Construction of the Wakefield Cycle (Carbondale: Southern Illinois University Press, 1974), pp. 28-30. In his interesting interpretation of the servant's speech, Gardner asserts that perceiving Cain as the devil becomes the "central, symbolic device of the play," p. 28. See also Gardner's essay, "Theme and Irony in the Wakefield Mactacio Abel," PMLA, 80 (1965), p. 517.

[19] Jeffrey, p. 69.

[20] It differs from other treatments as well, which stress Cain's doom at all times. As Donna Smith Vinter explains, often in the mystery plays "spiritual fate became character, their ends became their beginnings." In "Didactic Characterization: The Towneley Abraham," Comparative Drama, 14 (1980), 120. This kind of characterization is evident even as Cain is introduced in Cursor Mundi as "þe fendes fode / Was neuer wors of modir born." In Cursor Mundi, I, Richard Morris, ed. (1874; rpt. Early English Text Society, o.s. 57, London: Oxford University Press, 1961), Trinity MS., ll. 1056-57.

[21] Dorrel T. Hanks, Jr., "The Mactacio Abel and the Wakefield Cycle: A Study in Context," Southern Quarterly, 16 (1977), 52.

[22] Hanning argues that Cain's obsession with anality furthers low comedy as it links him with the devil (as presented, e.g., in the Summoner's Prologue and the Malacoda episode of Inferno XXI), pp. 32, 48.

[23] Eleanor Prosser, Drama and Religion in the English Mystery Plays: A Re-Evaluation (1961; rpt. Stanford: Stanford University Press, 1966), p. 81.

[24] Prosser, p. 78.

[25] T.W. Craik, "Violence in the English Mystery Plays," in Medieval Drama, Neville Denny, ed. (New York: Crane, Russak, & Company, Inc., 1973), p. 195.

[26] Jeffrey, p. 71.

[27] Millicent Carey points out that this focus on Cain's "rebellion against God because of his hard lot is unique . . . in medieval literature" and forms a theme for the entire play. In The Wakefield Group in the Towneley Cycle (Baltimore: The Johns Hopkins Press, 1930), p. 31.

[28] Carey, for example, says that "there is no humor in the main portion of the play" and that "the tone of the whole scene is almost tragic," p. 45. See also Blair W. Boone, "The Skill of Cain in the English Mystery Cycles," Comparative Drama, 16 (1982), 112-29; and Rosemary Woolf, The English Mystery Plays (1972; rpt. Berkeley: The University of California Press, 1973), pp. 127-29.

[29] Hartnett, p. 24.

[30] Hartnett, p. 25.

[31] Prosser, p. 78.

[32] For a convincing argument for the Wakefield Master's intentional use of varying levels of language to characterize contrasts in his plays, see Martin Stevens, "Language as Theme in the Wakefield Plays," Speculum, 52 (1977), 100-17.

[33] An example, Emerson suggests, is Cain's mention of "thystyls & brerys" (202), which is a reminder of his association with the man-in-the-moon story of popular legend, pp. 840-41. Such references--like the repetitions of devil in this play--are easily overlooked in the context of lively action.

[34] Kolve, p. 139.

[35] See Meyers, pp. 50-51; and Jeffrey, p. 69. Even John Gardner, whose approaches are usually insightful, argues that at first glance the spectators recognize Cain as a "devil's man in disguise" and never look beyond that first impression. In Construction of the Wakefield Cycle, p. 30.

[36] M.D. Anderson's reference to Cain in the Holkham Bible Picture Book is useful, for there the smoke from Cain's offering merges directly with the smoke that rises from hell-mouth. Other pictorial traditions of Cain show similar visual symbolism of his association with hell. In Drama and Imagery in English Medieval Churches, (1955; rpt. Cambridge: Cambridge University Press, 1963), p. 144.

[37] Woolf, p. 127.

[38] Honor Matthews, studying the myth of Cain and Abel as it emerges in Modern and Absurdist theater, remarks on the universality of "men's consciousness of guilt, fear of punishment and hope of redemption." In The Primal Curse: The Myth of Cain and

Abel in the Theatre (New York: Schocken Books, 1967), p. 11.

[39] Boone, p. 125.

[40] Boone, p. 125.

[41] Clifford Davidson finds that Cain "from the very start epitomizes . . . despair" and "represents the lapsarian principle" that foreshadows Judas' betrayal of Christ, p. 6.

[42] In a convincing presentation, Bennett A. Brockman demonstrates Cain's reliance on two distinct legal documents--the royal letter of protection and the royal letter of pardon--to justify his action, but "his mind is so constricted by the concerns of the earthly city that he is hardly aware of God's curse." In "The Law of Man and the Peace of God: Judicial Process as Satiric Theme in the Wakefield Mactacio Abel," Speculum, 49 (1974), 706.

[43] Brockman, p. 707.

[44] Woolf, p. 128.

[45] Stevens, working from a theory that the cycle plays were a showcase for craftsmen, proposes that the Noah play was included "first and foremost for the theatrical challenge that it provided for the Shipbuilders or Mariners who so often produced it," "Staging," p. 127.

[46] Nelson infers from the varying levels of stage loci that the pageant wagon theory fails to hold up; a central platea must have been present, with "scenic clusters" around it, pp. 133-36. See also Stevens, "Staging," pp. 123-27; and Cynthia Haldenby Tyson, "Noah's Flood, the River Jordan, the Red Sea: Staging in the Towneley Cycle," Comparative Drama, 8 (1974), 101-11.

[47] Tyson proposes that a trench or pit may have been used to channel water on stage, citing that the urgency of Noah's wife in boarding the ark would require vivid, realistic staging to convince the audience, pp. 102-06.

[48] See, for example, Holding, p. 54.

[49] Anderson, p. 40.

[50] Cursor Mundi, ll. 1634-42.

[51] Gardner, p. 42.

[52] "The Newcastle Play of Noah's Ark" (edited text), in Non-Cycle Plays and Fragments, Norman Davis and Osborn Waterhouse, eds. Early English Text Society, s.s. 1 (London: Oxford University Press, 1970), ll. 1-8. Subsequent references to the Newcastle play will be to this edition and cited by page numbers

in parentheses.

53 For a study of the traditions associated with Noah, see Don Cameron Allen, The Legend of Noah (Illinois Studies in Language and Literature, XXXIII, 3-4; Urbana: University of Illinois Press, 1949).

54 Dunn, p. 86.

55 Alan H. Nelson, "'Sacred' and 'Secular' Currents in The Towneley Play of Noah," Drama Survey, 3 (1964), 394.

56 Carey, p. 66.

57 Anna Jean Mill, "Noah's Wife Again," PMLA, 56 (1941), 613-26.

58 Mill, p. 615.

59 Mill, pp. 616-20.

60 Mill, p. 616.

61 For an overview of didactic literature--both religious and secular--concerned with women, see Alice A. Hentsch, De la Litterature Didactique du Moyen Age, s'adressant specialement aux femmes (Cambridge: Cahors, 1903). Hentsch includes primarily French, Italian, German, and English sources that present antifeminist references or models of virtue for women.

62 Tertullian, from De Cultu Feminarum, in Julia O'Faolain and Lauro Martines, eds., Not in God's Image: Women in History from the Greeks to the Victorians (London: Maurice Temple Smith Ltd., 1973), p. 132.

63 The Proverbs of Alfred, in An Old English Miscellany, Richard Morris, ed. (London, 1872, Early English Text Society o.s. 49; rpt. New York: Greenwood Press, 1969), 11. 269-80, 306-08, 323-28.

64 "In villa, in villa, quid vidistis in villa?" in Songs, Carols, and Other Miscellaneous Poems from the Balliol MS. 354, Richard Hill's Commonplace-Book, Roman Dyboski, ed. Early English Text Society, e.s. 101 (London: Oxford University Press, 1907), 11. 29-32, 45-56.

65 "Of All Creature Women Be Best . . ." in "Liedersammlungen des XVI. Jahrhunderts, besonders aus der Zeit Heinrichs VIII," III, Ewald Flügel, ed., Anglia, 26 (1903), 275-76.

66 "Hoow, Gossip Myne, Gossip Myn, Whan Will We Go to þe Wyne . . . ?" in Dyboski, 11. 61-66.

67 Gayley, p. 168. This study is typical of older criti-

cism, as he virtually ignores or shellacs the unsettling elements in the play, calling them "realistic touches, confidential asides, contemporary nicknames, assorted terms of abuse, and a rich, varied rustic philosophy," p. 168.

[68] Woolf, p. 143.

[69] Gardner, for example, identifies the most obvious level of meaning in the play: "as God chastises man for his bad behavior, Noah strives, mostly in vain, to chastise his wife," Construction of the Wakefield Cycle, p. 39.   See also Howard H. Schless, "The Comic Element in the Wakefield Noah," in Studies in Medieval Literature, in Honor of Professor Albert Croll Baugh, MacEdward Leach, ed. (Philadelphia: University of Pennsylvania Press, 1961), pp. 233-34.

[70] Stevens, seeing Noah as a man entrusted with divine law, asserts that the conflict between divine and civil law is "central to the Wakefield Author's dramatic vision. . . .   The civil law is constantly exposed for its abuses. . . .   It is usually the arrogant, self-aggrandizing, and loquacious tyrant figure who disturbs God's stillness with his ear-piercing harangues." In "Language as Theme," p. 110.

[71] See, for example, ballad 93 in Dyboski, pp. 110-11. Here a woman's loud complaining about something trivial causes her husband to beat her severely.   It closes with a warning to men to avoid such women,

> Lest he be knokken a-bowt þe pate;
> Then to repent yt ys to late,
> When on his cheke he ys chekmate,
>   [At þe townys end.]

[72] Carey, p. 96.

[73] An example of this attitude is in the Rules of Marriage compiled by Friar Cherubino of Siena in the fifteenth century: ". . . if your wife is of a servile disposition and has a crude and shifty spirit, so that pleasant words have no effect, scold her sharply, bully and terrify her.   And if this still doesn't work . . . take up a stick and beat her soundly, for it is better to punish the body and correct the soul than to damage the soul and spare the body. . . .   For example, if she blasphemes against God or a saint, if she mutters the devil's name, if she likes being at the window and lends a ready ear to dishonest young men, or if she has taken to bad habits or bad company, or commits some other wrong that is a mortal sin.   Then readily beat her, not in rage but out of charity and concern for her soul, so that the beating will redound to your merit and her good."   In O'Faolain and Martines, p. 177.

[74] Kolve, p. 150.

[75] Jeffrey, p. 75.

105

[76] Schless points out that the most important change is the dramatic treatment of Noah's wife, for she narrates every dramatic event while they are on board the ark, giving "voice to their renewed joy" and interpreting the signs of hope about them, p. 239.

[77] Nelson, "'Sacred' and 'Secular,'" p. 400.

[78] Robert L. Duncan, in defense of comedy in the Noah plays, argues that "the comic portions of the medieval plays were intended to divert the audience, not to subvert religious truth." In "Comedy in the English Mysteries: Three Versions of the Noah Story," Illinois Quarterly, 35 (1973), 11.

CHAPTER 3:
Comic Questioning of the Incarnation

The cycle plays which present the events surrounding the Nativity consistently develop the theme of faith in miracles, particularly the Incarnation. Instead of focusing attention directly on the central action--the birth of Christ--these plays first lead the spectators to the temple where Joseph was selected to become Mary's husband and to the hills outside Bethlehem. More than simple expansion of plot is at work here, for, in presenting a glimpse of the sacred event through such earthly eyes, the playwrights clearly intend that the spectators involve themselves directly in the characters' situations.

The central question here is difficult: how can men possibly accept the idea of Divine Incarnation, an article of faith which, in some sense, is more incomprehensible than the Resurrection?[1] In rational, human terms, this apparent paradox cannot be resolved or explained. For the cycle playwrights, such a perplexing mystery of faith presented unique challenges in dramaturgy. Traditional approaches--declarations of the need for Christ's coming and the prophecies which foretold it--would be insufficient dramatically within the context of the Corpus Christi cycles, and accepting the mystery as a given would reduce the plays to prayers spoken in parts.

Instead, the dramatists impose this bewildering question on the traditional Nativity narrative and seek answers not in the religious glosses but in the active human struggle men undergo to discover for themselves the meaning of these questions. In the best plays, this struggle is more than a complication for added interest: it becomes a battle that each spectator wages against himself, and the skillful dramatic resolution is an opportunity for personal acceptance as well.

Although the question itself is serious, the cycle playwrights use comedy as a dramatic device to involve the audience by "making low jest of high things."[2] The shepherds' plays, in particular, show some of the most intricate weaving of themes that one finds in the cycle plays. This study places that artistic achievement in a specific theological context: by placing difficult questions in the spectators' minds, by seeming to lead away from those questions through uproarious secular comedy, and by transforming dramatic intensity into religious intensity, the playwrights reveal a clear understanding of the way that humor can induce an audience to accept ideas that make sense only on an emotional level.

Joseph's Trouble about Mary

By the time the mystery cycles were written, well-known religious and secular works had long since experimented with the implications of Matthew I:19, the only passage which discusses Joseph's dilemma upon discovering that his betrothed is pregnant.[3] In the apocryphal gospels and extant sermons, one finds evidence for the medieval writers' interest in Joseph as he confronts the fact of Mary's pregnancy. Several of these, such as De Nativitate and Pseudo-Matthew, are cautious in their approaches; but the Protevangelium, an apocryphal gospel of

James, is characterized by "cynical realism" in the dialogue between Joseph and Mary.[4] The early English treatment--as seen, for example, in the Exeter Book--is evidence of continued interest in the human, domestic aspects of the miraculous conception. Critics agree that these sources, together with secular literature expounding the wretchedness of marriage, largely influenced the cycle playwrights' perceptions of Joseph.[5]

In each of the four major cycles and the Shearmen and Taylors' Pageant (a fragment of the true-Coventry cycle), Joseph appears as an old man who is dumbfounded by the discovery that Mary is pregnant. Although religious and secular sources suggest this characterization, the drama expands upon and exploits the material dramatically and transforms the scenes with Joseph into wild comic hilarity. Even the Chester Nativity--atypical of the usually sober cycle--presents him in this comic light, as he bemoans his situation to Elizabeth:

> Alas, alas, and woe is mee!
> Whoe hasse made her with chyld?
> Well I wist an ould man and a maye
> might not accord by noe waye.
> For many yeares might I not playe
> ne worke noe workes wild.
>
> Three monethes shee hath bine from mee.
> Now hasse shee gotten her, as I see,
> a great bellye like to thee
> syth shee went away.
> And myne yt is not, bee thow bould,
> for I am both ould and could;
> these xxx[tie] winters, though I would,
> I might not playe noe playe.

(123-36)

The York "Joseph's Trouble about Mary" echoes this sentiment, as Joseph dodders alone complaining of his age:

> For I am of grete elde,

110

```
Wayke and al vnwelde,
    Als ilke man se it maye;
I may nowder buske ne belde,
But owther in frith or felde;
    For shame what sall I saie

That þus-gates nowe on myne alde dase
Has wedded a yonge wenche to my wiff,
And may noȝt wele tryne over two strase!
```
$$(5-13)$$

Such passages, which emphasize Joseph's age from the perspective of his marriage to a young woman, hint at the sexual implications of such a match without developing them. The Chester dramatist plays lightly with the obvious joke of the cuckolded husband by having Joseph harangue about the woes of marriage. Although his monologue opens like a prayer addressed to God, Joseph is speaking more to the audience, warning the men there not to repeat his mistake:

```
God, lett never [an] ould man
take to wife a yonge woman
ney seet his harte her upon,
lest hee beguyled bee.
For accorde ther maye be none,
ney the may never bee at one;
and that is seene in manye one
as well as one mee.
```
$$(145-52)$$

The mention of the word "beguyled" here indicates that something other than "usual" female deceit is responsible for the discord in their marriage. Instead of expanding this explanation, however, the Chester playwright quickly allows an angel to intercede, and Joseph ceases his grumbling when he hears that "this is Godes will" (164).[6]

The York and Towneley plays, on the other hand, develop more directly the implications of cuckoldry in Christ's conception, encouraging the spectators to perceive Joseph as the brunt of some great divine joke. In both of the plays, Joseph knows the prophecy of Christ's birth but rejects it, in York because he cannot believe that Mary would be chosen, and in Towneley because he cannot believe that he ". . . is worthi to be / That blyssed body besyde" (318-19). He limits himself to human, earthly interpretations of the event, and he responds on this most basic level. In the York play, for example, Joseph becomes a raging, jealous husband as he directly accuses Mary of lying:

> Þanne se I wele youre menyng is,
> Þe Aungell has made hir with childe.
> Nay, som man in aungellis liknesse
> With somkyn gawde has hir begiled;
> And þat trow I.
> For-thy nedes noght swilke wordis wilde
> At carpe to me dissayuandly.
> We! why gab ye me swa
> and feynes swilk fantassy,
> Allas! me is full wa!
> for dule why ne myght I dy.
>
> . . .
>
> Allas! why wrought þou swa,
> Marie! my weddid wiffe?
>
> (134-55)

Joseph is a type of the deceived husband here, reacting both with anger and with shame to his discovery of Mary's pregnancy. More irritating to him than her deception, however, is her insistence that an angel, not a man, cuckolded him. In his reference to "som man in aungellis liknesse," Joseph categorizes Mary's explanation as a typical lame excuse. The spectators would recognize his unknowing reference to the fabliaux and be surprised to discover it here.[7]

The Towneley presentation also develops the idea that

Joseph was deceived, for here the description of age is colored by the sexual decrepitude of the old man:

> I irke full sore with my lyfe,
> That euer I wed so yong a wyfe,
>   That bargan may I ban;
> To me it was a carefull dede,
> I myght well wyt that yowthede
>   wold haue lykyng of man.
>
> I am old, sothly to say,
> passed I am all preuay play,
>   The gams fro me ar gane.
> It is ill cowpled of youth and elde;
> I wote well, for I am vnwelde,
>   som othere has she tane.

                                        (161-72)

The Towneley Joseph, like the character in York, seems to share the _fabliau_ tradition with his audience when he generalizes about the unfortunate results that occur when an old man takes a young wife. This tradition, however, is used quite differently in the two plays. Whereas the York character becomes angry when he assumes his wife is like the women in the tales, the Towneley Joseph comically resigns himself to the fact that women cannot be faithful. His lament, then, is less an outpouring of the wounds he feels than a sigh that Mary is like all others:

> Shuld an angell this dede haue wroght?
> Sich excusyng helpys noght,
>   ffor no craft that thay can;
> A heuenly thyng, for sothe, is he,
> And she is erthly; this may not be,
>   It is som othere man.
>
> Certys, I forthynk sore of hir dede,
> Bot it is long of yowth-hede,
>   All sich wanton playes;
> ffor yong women wyll nedys play them
> with yong men, if old forsake them,
>   Thus it is sene always.
>
> Bot marie and I playd neuer so sam,
> Neuer togeder we vsid that gam,
>   I cam hir neuer so nere;

>   she is as clene as cristall clyfe
>   ffor me, and shalbe whyls I lyf,
>   The law wyll it be so.
>   And then am I cause of hir dede,
>   ffor thi then can I now no rede,
>   Alas, what I am wo!

(293-313)

Although one may see Joseph as a victim of fate here, the fact that Joseph only imagines his cuckoldry suggests a more comic effect. He is _not_ the beguiled husband he thinks he is, and the careful logic he uses to determine that Mary must have had an earthly lover is laughable because he goes through such throes to explain the irrational (or supra-rational) in such rational, worldly terms. The personal torment Joseph suffers to arrive at a reconciliation with Mary--and with God[8]--is gently comic here, for the playwright works to maintain the irony which distances his audience from the central character. The Towneley spectators are not lured to take Joseph's doubts to heart, for they are often reminded--in such directly ironic comments as "It is som othere man"--that they have knowledge of the truth that the character himself lacks. On a dramatic level, the spectators can enjoy the doubts because they have the truth; they can play with the misunderstanding because they are confident in their knowledge.

The dramatic situation of the Towneley play is concise and unified, and, as Eleanor Prosser argues, a significant development over the longer York play.[9] Yet the most emotionally stirring treatment of Joseph's doubts occurs in the N-Town play, _Joseph's Return_. This version succeeds, where others do not, in its attempts to involve the spectators in the action, to encourage them in their own struggles with the religious concept of Divine Incarnation. Not coincidentally, this play is also the most clearly comic version in the cycles.

When Prosser summarizes critical attitudes toward the N-Town play, her own view that its comedy has little relation to the subject matter is echoed in this comment:

> Critical rejection has been general: the play is too long, unnecessarily coarse, and--in contrast to other Hegge plays--wholly secular. Its only saving grace is thought to be its realism, the element that at the same time makes the play thoroughly repellent.[10]

Yet the elements of coarse "realism" which Prosser finds so repugnant are precisely the sources of dramatic energy which distinguish this play from others on the subject. More than any other cycle or the true-Coventry fragment, the N-Town treatment of Joseph's problem is an intense working out of the question of the Incarnation.

One of the most striking features of the play is the highly devotional context in which it is placed. Perhaps if this play--with its full development of the secular comedy implicit in Joseph's dilemma--were to appear as part of the Wakefield Master's canon, its vulgarity would not be as startling as in the midst of several plays clearly written in praise of Mary.[11] It is this very context, however, which gives the play its dramatic strength: after the narration of prophecies, after the long history of Mary's conception and youth, and after the highly symbolic presentation of the Annunciation, the playwright

115

deliberately moves to an examination of the secular response to one of the most important events in religious history. Without such a context, the play would be only a well-wrought incorporation of _fabliau_ material into religious narrative; within this context, the dynamic struggle between divine intention and earthly understanding is intensified, and the spectators gain a firmer grasp on the irrational mystery through the dramatic presentation of earthly and rational doubting.

The conception of Christ is presented concisely and emotionally in _Salutation and Conception,_ the play which precedes _Joseph's Return._ The action is treated only as part of the angel Gabriel's narrative in the other cycles, not as an event presented on stage. For example, the Towneley _Annunciation_ presents the action only by discussing it as a future event, presumably occurring off stage:

> _Gabriell._ lady, this is the preuate;
> Thy holy gost shall light in the,
>   And his vertue,
> he shall vmshade and fulfyll
> That thi madynhede shall neuer spyll,
>   Bot ay be new.
>
> (125-30)[12]

The N-Town treatment, however, succeeds in presenting the action of conception explicitly on stage without becoming humorous or obscene. The stage direction following line 292 suggests a symbolic representation of the conception, one in which "iij bemys. . . entre. . . to here bosom."[13] More important than the actual presentation of the Incarnation on stage is Mary's reaction to the event. Her words attest to her humility and her joy in serving God without denying the physical and emotional ful-

116

fillment that such an occurrence would bring:

A now I ffele in my body be
parfyte god and parfyte man
havyng Al schappe   of chyldly carnalyte
Evyn Al at onys   þus god be-gan.

Nott takynge ffyrst o membyr and sythe A-nother
but parfyte childhod ȝe haue A-non
of ·ȝour hand-mayden   now ȝe haue mad ȝour modyr
With-owte peyne in Fflesche and bon
Thus conceyved nevyr woman non
þat evyr was beynge in þis lyff
O myn hyest ffadyr in ȝour tron
It is worthy ȝour son   now my son   haue A
                                    prerogatyff.

I can not telle what joy what blysse
now I fele in my body
Aungel Gabryel I thank ȝow for thys
most mekely recomende me   to my faderys mercy
To haue be þe modyr of god fful lytyl wend I
Now myn cosyn Elyzabeth ffayn wold I se
how sche hath conseyvid as ȝe dede specyfy
Now blyssyd be þe hyȝ trynyte.

(293-312)

Such a speech presents Mary in the best possible light, for she
reacts both as a devout servant, pleased to do God's work, and
as a young mother, already taking pride and pleasure in the
child she has just conceived. The closing prayer of Gabriel
continues this joyful tone, appropriately ending with "An Ave
new" (339).

When Joseph appears on stage in the following play, this
high spirituality is immediately brought to its lowest level:
the Ave of the preceding play is inverted, in Joseph's mind, to
the treachery of Eva.[14] Having already established in The
Betrothal of Mary that Joseph is a weak, "Almost lame" (228) old
man who suspects that "it is a straunge thynge An old man to
take a ȝonge wyff" (182), the N-Town playwright allows for a

full dramatic expansion of the suggestion that Joseph has been deceived. This development, Woolf suggests, moves in two directions at once, for Mary's elevation is concomitant with Joseph's debasement:

> While theologically the pattern of the first and second Eve is made complete at the Annunciation, the dramatists have contrived that the climax should be extended to the plays of Joseph's Doubts: this they have achieved by bringing the two worlds of Fall and Redemption into a dramatic collision. Doctrinally Joseph's doubts serve by ironic reversal to emphasize that the Virgin is the second Eve, and for this reason the Ludus Coventriae, which had most exalted the role of the Blessed Virgin, also most elaborates (even to the point of obscenity) Joseph's conviction that he has been deceived.[15]

This collision is developed on a dramatic, as well as doctrinal level, for Joseph's actions immediately establish a sharp contrast to the gentle singing and praise of the previous play. He bangs loudly on the bolted door, shouting commands with explicitly sexual overtones:

How dame how vn-do ȝoure dore vn-do Are ȝe at hom why speke ȝe notht	Joseph
Who is ther why cry ȝe so telle us ȝour herand wyl ȝe ought.	Susanna
Vn-do ȝour dore I sey ȝow to Ffor to com in is all my thought.	Joseph

(1-6)

Such a violent opening signals two important differences from the play which precedes Joseph's Return: the dramatist develops, from the outset, an active--rather than contemplative--tone which dominates the play; and he deliberately invites the spectators to think of the Incarnation in the base human terms worked out comically in the fabliaux.[16] This interest in the

118

popular stories of the cuckolded husband serves as more than just an occasional source of dramatic humor, for clearly the _fabliau_ tradition seems

> to have suggested to . . . [the playwright] the
> basic form which the Joseph materials were to
> take under his hand, namely, that of the cuck-
> olded husband fabliau.[17]

This form also leads the spectators to anticipate a specific sequence of events as soon as they see Joseph, the betrayed husband, returning unexpectedly.

Once he is allowed to enter the house, Joseph reveals through his dialogue with Mary that his role of _senex amans_ is to be played consistently. In his own mind, his fears that "an old man may nevyr thryff / with a ȝonge wyff" (_The Betrothal of Mary_, 278-79) are realized here, for he knows immediately that something is changed. The brightness of Mary's face--in accordance with iconographic association of light with the Virgin[18]-- prevents Joseph from seeing her. Joseph demonstrates a blindness which is both characteristic of the _fabliau_ tradition and symbolic of the spiritual blindness he is to exhibit later in the play.[19]

His words are charged with irony: he attributes her glow to "þe sonne with his bemys" (16), not realizing, of course, that the Son of the Trinity is the actual source of light. His greeting, "How hast þou ferde jentyl mayde / whyl I haue be out of londe" (21-22), recalls his earlier warnings that she remain chaste:

> But fayr maydon I þe pray
> Kepe þe clene as I xal me
> I am a man of age

                            119

         therfore sere busshop I wyl þat ʒe wete
         þat in bedde we xul nevyr mete
         Ffor i-wys mayden suete
         An Old man may not rage.

                          . . .

         þis ix monthis þou seyst me nowth
         Kepe þe clene my jentyl spowse
         and all þin maydenys in þin howse
         þat evyl langage I here not rowse
         Ffor hese love þat all hath wrought.
              (The Betrothal of Mary, 291-97, 469-73)

The fact that he even asks such a loaded question upon his

return reveals his conviction that Mary is like the deceitful

women of the fabliaux.

    In a delightful bit of repartee which plays at once with

fabliau conventions and religious mysteries, Mary's responses,

while truthful, are shrouded in ambiguity that lends itself to

misinterpretation. Such equivocation, as in the following

lines, is another feature of the typical fabliau structure:[20]

         Sekyr sere beth nowth dysmayde
         Ryth aftyr þe wyl of goddys sonde.
                                        (23-24)

A game is thus established between the husband and wife, in

which Joseph persistently asks accusing questions, and Mary

defends herself with answers that make sense only to those who

know the whole story. Whereas in the fabliaux, discovery of

specific evidence forces the lovers to complicate their strate-

gies in order to confound the husband, Mary needs only to tell

the truth to convince Joseph that she has betrayed him. Joseph

reacts as if he has been expecting just such a response:

         I drede me sore I am be-trayd
         Sum other man þe had in honde
         Hens sythe þat I went
         Thy Wombe is gret it gynnyth to ryse

120

> than hast þou be-gownne a synfull gyse
> telle me now in what wyse
> thy self þou Ast þus schent.
>
> Ow dame what þinge menyth this
> with childe þou gynnyst ryth gret to gon
> Sey me mary þis childys fadyr ho is
> I pray þe telle me and þat anon.
>
> (27-42)

Joseph, unlike his weak counterparts in the other cycles, reacts with the rage that the audience has been led to expect. His declaration, "Goddys childe þou lyist in fay" (43), sounds as much like an anachronistic curse on his wife as a denunciation of her excuse; and his angry statement that "God dede nevyr jape so with may" (44) reveals that he is tired of Mary's games.

The lament that ensues is more direct in its appeal to the spectators than that in any of the other cycles.[21] Although this self-pity, and its generalized criticism of marriage, is a feature of all treatments of Joseph in the plays, here the fact of Mary's pregnancy supports the critical asides that Joseph had mentioned in The Betrothal of Mary. In the following lines are several instances of the speaker's self-mockery, comic here because the spectators are never allowed to forget that Mary is not deceptive. The tone, however, is not entirely comic, and Joseph's decision to leave his wife does not seem as cruel or illogical as in the other plays:

> ȝa ȝa all Olde men to me take tent
> and weddyth no wyff in no kynnys wyse
> þat is a ȝonge wench be myn a-sent
> ffor doute and drede and swych servyse
> Alas Alas my name is shent
> all men may me now dyspyse
> and seyn olde cokwold þi bow is bent
> newly now after þe frensche gyse
> Alas and welaway
> Alas dame why dedyst þou so

121

```
Ffor þis synne þat þou hast do
I the for-sake and from þe go
Ffor onys evyr and Ay.
```

                                        (49-61)

Although Prosser describes Joseph as "a cantankerous lout,

. . . wallowing in self-pity,"[22] the expanded developments of

the previous plays add depth to his misery. He is pitiable, to

the audience as well as to himself, for the very fears he ac-

knowledged during the betrothal scene seem to have been real-

ized: Mary is undeniably pregnant, and he feels betrayed and

ashamed.

Unlike the other cycles and Nicholas Love's <u>Mirrour of the</u>

<u>Blessed Lyf of Jesu Christ</u> (generally considered an important

source for this play),[23] the N-Town play has Mary offer a full

explanation to Joseph. Her once equivocal answers, such as

"this childe is goddys and ȝour" (42), give way to this more

direct tatement:

```
It is no man but swete jhesus
he wyll be clad in flesch and blood
and of ȝour wyff be born.
```

                                        (64-66)

The problem here is that, in Joseph's eyes, Mary is still tell-

ing riddles. The answer that the audience knows to be true

begins to sound more and more like the complicated kind of lie a

deceitful wife might make. In his angry accusations, in his

suggestion that the sin itself is made more horrible by Mary's

lying about an accomplice,[24] and in his insistence that some

cruel game is being played around him, Joseph reveals the seri-

ousness with which he doubts:

```
An Aungel allas alas fy for schame
ȝe syn now in þat ȝe to say
```

122

```
    to puttyn an Aungel in so gret blame
    Alas alas let be do way
    It was sum boy be-gan þis game
    þat clothyd was clene and gay
    and ȝe ȝeve hym now an Aungel name
    Alas alas and wel away
    þat evyr this game be-tydde
    A dame what thought haddyst þou
    Here may all men þis proverbe trow
    þat many a man doth bete þe bow
    Another man hath þe brydde.
```
                                              (71-83)

The dramatic situation also becomes more serious, for the old
man--in spite of his comic raving and bungling--points to an
important question about the Incarnation: why, when all physical
evidence is against Mary, should anyone believe her story? By
criticizing Mary's attempt to blame an angel for her fault,
Joseph reveals that he does not weigh the question in anything
but rational, human terms; and, by this standard, she is clearly
lying.

Were Joseph's Return merely an enjoyable interlude within a
body of devotional Marian plays, the suggestion of Mary's deceit
could be brushed aside as the playwright's whimsical treatment
of a senseless old man. This play, however, alludes to the
religious significance of Joseph's doubt often enough to reveal
that the comic portions of the play are used to serious ends.
Gibson argues that the iconographic tradition of the porta
clausa--Ezekiel's vision of the closed door which symbolizes
"miraculously inviolate childbirth"[25]--is deliberately introduced in the N-Town Annunciation scene and remains foremost in
the spectators' minds as they witness Joseph's Return. Gibson's
evidence from visual arts of the Middle Ages supports her asser-

123

tions that the closed-door motif is well established in the context of the cycle by the time Joseph orders Mary to "Vn-do oure dore." Denying the importance of the _fabliau_ tradition, Gibson assumes that distant reverence was the reaction of the audience:

> . . . it is difficult to see how Joseph's persis-
> tent knocking at a locked door would not have
> struck responsive chords even in the simplest
> member of a medieval audience witnessing a play
> about Mary's pregnancy. . . . The comedy of
> Joseph's impatience before that locked door en-
> closing the Virgin is not _fabliau_ so much as
> remarkably inventive translation of the _porta
> clausa_ mystery in this dramatic action. . . .
> Certainly the thrice-repeated commandment to open
> the door has Trinitarian significance in a mys-
> tery cycle which placed such emphasis upon the
> participation of the entire Trinity in the in-
> carnation.[26]

Although evidence in the text supports such devotional motiva-tion on the part of the N-Town playwright, one may easily invert Gibson's argument, suggesting that even the most sophisticated member of a medieval audience could not ignore the obvious low comedy of the scene. The resolution of such apparently conflic-ting views is the source of dramatic and theological strength of this play: the dramatist juggles religious and coarsely comic associations so that the audience is asked to respond simulta-neously to the farce and the devotional story. What appears, on the surface, to be a random flurry of opposites is actually a carefully designed plan to give the appearance of disorder. Especially within the devotional context of this cycle, such disorder is both disruptive and attractive; more importantly, it forces a kind of spectator involvement which differs from the

124

earlier plays of this cycle.

Repentance, several critics agree, is the theme of the plays about Joseph and the particular emphasis of the N-Town treatment.[27] Prosser maintains that Joseph is initially characterized in repulsive terms precisely so that his repentance will appear all the more striking:

> The later Joseph is a new man, inconsistent with his former self and thus unbelievable. Exactly. He is a "new man." The "old man," Adam, has been suddenly washed away by the mystery of divine grace. . . . There is perhaps no mystery of the Christian religion more difficult for modern man to accept, but we must understand it if we are to judge contemporary reaction to medieval and Renaissance drama.[28]

What is left unexplained in this statement, however, is the dramatist's reason for shaping the character of Joseph in such explicitly comic terms. The playwright need not have characterized Joseph as the cuckolded husband in order to evince the marked contrast Prosser discusses.[29] One may conclude that the decision to parallel the fabliaux was based as much on its dramatic as its thematic advantages.

A close examination of the play itself reveals the dramatic effects of such purposefully comic development. The enjoyment for the audience at the opening of the play is based primarily on a skillfully crafted situation of dramatic irony: the spectators, aware of both the biblical narrative and the fabliau tradition, know more about Joseph than he himself does. They know that what Mary says is the truth, but the direct confrontation of reason and mystery is comic and engaging.

This dramatic situation becomes more complex, however, when

125

Joseph continues his questions. Although casting him in the role of the _senex amans_ does round out the character in an enjoyable way, this development also complicates the traditional narrative. Typically, _fabliaux_ in the cuckolded husband tradition end with a scene of joyful reunion:

> The husband is so completely taken in by the wily stratagem or sufficient answer that he is fully convinced of the fidelity of his wife and is often overjoyed at the outcome. He frequently also feels the need to apologize for missaying or misdoing.[30]

Because this play so closely parallels the _fabliaux_, one anticipates a similar handling of the play's conclusion. Such an explanation, however, is difficult on religious grounds. In the _fabliaux_, the ironic situation continues because the husband becomes convinced--mistakenly and, therefore, comically--that what he originally saw or heard was not what actually occurred; in _Joseph's Return,_ the playwright must work to overcome the spectators' growing hunch that Joseph was similarly hoodwinked. A complex double vision results, for the audience is asked to recognize Joseph as a type of the cuckolded husband and--at the same time--to realize that he has not, in fact, been beguiled by Mary.

Sympathy for Joseph builds in this play because so much attention is fixed on him. Because Joseph does not have knowledge of Mary's pregnancy when the play begins (as in the other cycles), the dramatic emphasis is on his reaction to the apparently flimsy explanations he receives. Moreover, this play, much like the Towneley _Annunciation_, is structured in such a way as to place emphasis on the basic, human response to the incomprehensible fact of Incarnation.[31] The playwright keeps his stress--relentlessly--on Joseph as man and betrayed husband. Thus despite the lack of wits his age suggests (fully developed in the other plays), and despite his wild tirades, he remains a rational, worldly wise man. Indeed, his knowledge of human nature and the inevitable treachery of young wives gives him the appearance of worldly wisdom, but he simultaneously reveals his foolishness in understanding the divine context. The wisdom he has is wildly inappropriate in relation to the divine, and it allows him only a rigid, limited logic which disallows the possibility that Mary is telling the truth:

> Nay nay ȝet god ffor-bede
> þat I xuld do þat vegeabyl dede
>   but if I wyst wel qwy
> I knew never with here so god me spede
> tokyn of thynge is word nor dede
>   þat towchyd velany
> nevyr þe les what for thy
> þow she be meke and mylde
> With-owth mannys company
> she myght not be with childe.

(98-107)

His syllogism makes perfect sense in ordinary human situations: pregnancy results from "mannys company"; Mary is pregnant; therefore, one must conclude that Mary followed the usual course to conception. Joseph knows from the prophecies that another possibility might exist, just as the spectators know from biblical history and from the preceding plays that an angel did, in fact, appear to Mary. But the _fabliau_ context and logical structure playfully develop the possibility of doubt. This is the dramatic center of the play toward which the dramatist has

127

moved.

For Joseph, the result is despair, as he turns to the audience for sympathy: "All men haue pety on me amonge / Ffor to my sorwe is no chere" (125-26). This confusion and hopelessness provide the exact situation in which true repentance can occur. When over-rationalizing brings only bewilderment, one not only becomes receptive to other possibilities, but actively seeks answers by changing one's mode of perception. Joseph wanders alone, but Mary's intercession--a feature unique to this play-- becomes dramatically and theologically necessary.

Although on three occasions before this critical point in the play, Mary has told Joseph what is necessary to accept her story as truth, her advice to "amende ȝour mon" (41) is lost when he focuses instead on the physical implications of her condition. Joseph's concentration on what Mary is _not_ saying prevents him from hearing what is most obvious in her speech. The spectators' anticipation and enjoyment of the fully devel- oped _fabliau_ also diverts their attention from her simple in- struction.

The audience always maintains its double vision and sees that another form of perception is possible, but Joseph is riveted in his despair securely enough to doubt even the pres- ence of an angel. The angel jolts him from this narrow per- spective, however, by revealing the sense of awe one needs to understand the miracle of the Incarnation:

> In þi wepynge þou dost ryght ylle
> A-ȝens god þou hast mys-wrought
> Go chere þi wyff with herty wylle
> and chawnge þi chere Amende þi thought

128

> Sche is a ful clene may
> I telle þe god wyl of here be born
> And sche clene mayd as she was be-forn
> to saue mankynd þat is for-lorn
> Go chere hyre þerfore I say.
>
> (151-59)

Because Joseph, at last, is willing to look beyond his limited logic, the same explanation that Mary offered now makes sense. Once he recognizes the way in which he "mys-wrought"--his willful doubting of the miracle by working from only the rational, human context--Joseph has already begun the most important aspect of repentance. Instead of reinforcing the impression that he has been deceived--as one sees in the traditional _fabliaux_--this play concludes with reassurance that, at last, Joseph is not misled by his own limited perception.

It is surely for this reason that the N-Town playwright lyrically emphasizes Joseph's great joy in discovering his own mistake. Although his relief and his rapid change of heart toward Mary seem comic at first,[32] the length of the passage following the angel's visit allows this humor to work its full course. Having toyed with the idea that the Divine Conception might possibly have been an elaborately designed ruse, the playwright allows Joseph's exuberant "A lord god benedicite" (160) to signal that the game is now over. Joseph criticizes his own narrow vision, and his lavish appeals for Mary's forgiveness celebrate repentance in its most positive state:

> I know wel I haue myswrought
> I walk to my pore place
> And Aske ffor-gyfnes I haue mys-thought.
>
> Now is þe tyme sen At eye
> þat þe childe is now to veryfye
> which xal saue mankende

As it was spoke be prophesye
I thank þe god þat syttys on hye
    with hert wyl and mende
þat evyr þou woldyst me bynde
to wedde mary to my wyff
þi blysful sone so nere to fynde
In his presens to lede my lyff.

Alas ffor joy I qwedyr and qwake
Alas what hap now was this
A mercy mercy my jentyl make
mercy I haue seyd al Amys
All þat I haue sayd here I for-sake
    our swete fete now lete my kys.

              (167-85)

From this stance, Joseph can see the whole picture clearly. In the other cycles, once this vision is established, the resolution of the play is very rapid. For example, in Towneley, Joseph confesses, "I haue trespast to god and the" (357); in the fifteen lines that follow, Mary readily forgives him and the play is ended. A similar pattern is evident in the Chester play, where Joseph drives out his "feeble thought" (161) by acknowledging, "A, nowe I wott, lord, yt is soe" (169). In the N-Town play, however, the resolution focuses more on the type of change that Joseph--and all men of faith--must undergo. If he is to participate in the mystery, he must listen from his "pore place," a stance which admits that human reason is incapable of understanding or explaining divine mystery. The visual presentation of Joseph at Mary's feet--instead of his banging on the door--reinforces this repentant stance.

The dramatist could not have achieved this intimate, joyful resolution without the comic frame of the play. Because of the careful weaving of the _fabliau_ tradition into the biblical narrative, the spectators are immediately involved in the fun of the fast-paced, familiar story they witness in the context of the supreme divine mystery. This emotional involvement is maintained when the central character begins to take his doubts seriously, for the spectators have reached an intensity of laughter which does not diminish when the play shifts levels. The dramatic and comic treatment of the limitations of human reason encourages the spectators to examine playfully their own doubts. The dramatic resolution thus offers a thematic and personal one as well, for in Joseph's repentance and in his acceptance of the miracle, the play reinforces the idea that each person has the capacity to amend himself. The repetition of the entire story is in a different tone from before, for, in closing, the intensity grows out of renewed understanding and faith.

The Shepherds and Other Doubters

The problem of understanding what Divine Incarnation means is extended in the cycles beyond the limited sphere of the family circle to include the doubts of shepherds, midwives, and earthly rulers. In such a shift, the question itself changes considerably. Whereas Joseph is initially caught up in the personal implications of such an event--thinking more about Mary's assumed deception than the miracle of Christ's imminent birth--the doubters in the other plays surrounding the Nativity question the implied promise of redemption in that birth. In several of the cycles, the anachronisms make clear that this miracle should be seen as more than an historical event. The

131

playwright thus underlines the point that the process by which the characters come to acknowledge and accept the presence of God among them is one in which the spectators, too, must become involved.

As in the plays of Joseph, the dramatic movement is from earthly enjoyment to intensified, joyous affirmation of faith.[33] And here, too, a condition for achieving that end is the involvement of the audience in the characters' uncertainty. Because of the comic developments which sometimes raucously share the stage with the holy event of the Nativity, the spectators become immersed in the bold human drama, thus temporarily losing sight of the greater spiritual drama. These comic frames establish not only the need for man's redemption--the crude state of the world at the time of Christ's birth--but, more importantly, the very means by which men are to see beyond that unpolished context to the divine miracle.

Only the York cycle moves away from the treatment of human doubt once Joseph's fears are allayed. In that cycle, humble, devout shepherds appear on stage only to summarize the prophecies of Hosea and Isaiah and to offer their simple gifts.[34] The other cycles, however, move from a confirmation of Joseph's faith to an examination of the Incarnation from other perspectives. The N-Town _Trial of Joseph and Mary_, for example, includes the scene in which Mary has to defend herself. Her accusers attack precisely those issues which Joseph had found to be illogical. The difference lies in the dramatic response demanded of the audience, for those who criticize her are the objects of laughter.

The summoner's prologue to the play is characterized by references to contemporary, rather than biblical, people and events. As he lists the names of those who are summoned to court, his speech rings with fifteenth-century allusions:

> Thom tynkere and betrys belle
> peyrs pottere and whatt at þe welle
> Symme Smalfeyth and kate kelle
>   and bertylmew þe bochere
> kytt cakelere and colett crane
> gylle fetyse and fayr jane
> powle pewterere and pernel prane
>   and phelypp þe good flecchere.
>   (13-20)

The style of this passage--its alliteration, bouncing rhythm, and song-like end rhymes--encourages a comic response to the long list of wrongdoers. In addition to eliciting laughter, such an address to the audience has two important dramatic functions. If the actor playing the summoner were to move among the spectators, as suggested in his speech, pointing and muttering his threats in asides to individuals, this prologue would serve as an appropriate preparation for the play. The members of the audience are herded up, like "Malkyn mylkedoke" (10) and "letyce lytyl trust" (22) to direct their attention toward the action about to occur. Particularly if there were no break between this and the previous play, the speech also serves to relax the audience without losing the control that the actors must maintain. More importantly, however, this speech is a comic rendering of an important theme in the play to follow: the superficiality of earthly judgment.

The summoner admits that the financial situation of a

person brought to court is the only basis on which his case is tried: "And loke ȝe rynge wele in ȝour purs / Ffor ellys ȝour cawse may spede þe wurs" (25-26). These satirical comments on medieval courts offer an amusing release for the spectators. But the description of the judicial process that the audience knows well also establishes an important context for the trial. Before they even glimpse the detractors who accuse Mary, the spectators anticipate the kind of rough handling that they have seen in fifteenth-century England. The detractors are thus cast as antagonists, whose misinterpretations of the Incarnation are enjoyable to the knowledgeable audience.

Before Mary and Joseph are summoned to court, the detractors reveal themselves as allegorical representations of evil. As one critic suggests, their "speeches belong to the dramatic tradition of Devil and Vice in their combination of malice and a gleeful, racy idiom."[35] One announces that "to reyse slawdyr is al my lay" (7), and the other avers: "If I may reyse þer with de-bate / I xal not spare þe seyd to sowe" (39-40). Here, unlike in Joseph's Return, the doubts are spoken by personified abstractions of evil, who discredit their own arguments by emphasizing their malicious design. Although the following speech echoes more explicitly the kind of doubts that Joseph himself had, here the obscene references to Mary turn the laughter on the unwitting speakers:

ijus detractor
ȝa þat old shrewe joseph my trowth I plyght
was so Anameryd upon þat mayd
þat of hyre bewte whan he had syght
He sesyd nat tyll had here a-sayd.

                                              1us detractor
    A nay nay wel wers she hath hym payd
    Sum fresch ʒonge galaunt she loveth wel more
    þat his leggys to here hath leyd
    and þat doth greve þe old man sore.

                                             ij^us detractor
    be my trewth al may wel be
    ffor fresch and fayr she is to syght
    And such a mursel as semyth me
    Wolde cause A ʒonge man to haue delyght.

                                              1us detractor
    Such a ʒonge damesel of bewte bryght
    And of schap so comely Also
    Of hire tayle ofte tyme be lyght
    and rygh tekyl vndyr þe too.

                                              (49-64)

These scurrilous comments are comic in the sense that the
devil's limited vision is laughable, and the audience--instead
of participating in the challenge here--is spurred to distance
itself from these buffoons. To ensure that such a stance is
maintained, the N-Town playwright presents the summoner once
more. As he performs his duty in bringing Mary and Joseph to
court, the summoner presumably moves through the audience,
directing threats and insults at members of the crowd:

    A-wey serys lete me com nere
    A man of wurchep here comyth to place
    of curtesy me semyth ʒe be to lere
    Do of ʒour hodys with an evyl grace.

    Do me sum wurchep be-for my face
    or be my trowth I xal ʒow make
    If þat I rolle ʒow up in my race
    Ffor fere I xal do ʒour ars qwake

    But ʒit sum mede and ʒe me take
    I wyl with-drawe my gret rough toth
    gold or sylvyr I wol not for-sake
    but evyn as all somnorys doth.

                                              (117-28)

The contemporary references to corrupted summoners encourage the spectators to perceive the detractors and their system of inquiry and judgment in the same satiric light that they view their own courts. By bringing Mary and Joseph on stage after such careful dramatic structuring, the dramatist allows his audience to celebrate the fact that, at last, those in power will be overcome.

The sarcasm with which the summoner and detractors address the accused couple thus serves only to illustrate their own lack of knowledge. The audience enjoys passages such as the following, always confident that a final coup de grace will humble the arrogant speaker:

```
Ther-fore com forth cokewolde be name
þe busschop xal ʒour lyff appose
Com forth Also ʒe goodly dame
A clene huswyff as I suppose
I xal ʒow tellyn with-owtyn glose.
and ʒe were myn with owtyn lak
I wolde ech day be-schrewe ʒour nose
and ʒe dede brynge me such a pak.
```

(153-60)

Even the bishop, who is related to Mary, doubts her story once he sees her, for the obvious physical evidence outweighs her assertion that "of ffleschly lust and gostly wownde / In dede nere thought I nevyr a-sayd" (179-80). Just as in the earlier scenes with Joseph, the declarations of the truth are overlooked by those who choose to misinterpret them; the difference is that the spectators, having already resolved this problem for themselves, confidently watch others falter.

In spite of the fact that Joseph has drunk the "botel of goddys vengeauns" (201)[36] and should be believed, the accusers dwell on his weakness instead of his strength:

136

Den

```
This olde shrewe may not wele gon
longe he taryeth to go A-bowth
lyfte up þi feet sett forth þi ton
or be my trewth þou getyst a clowte.
```

ij^{us} detractor

```
now sere evyl Thedom com to þi snowte
What heylyght þi leggys now to be lame
þou dedyst hem put ryght freschly owte
Whan þou dedyst pley with ȝon ȝonge dame.
```

1 detractor

```
I pray to god gyf hym myschawns
hese leggys here do folde for Age
but with þis damysel whan he dede dawns
þe olde charle had ryght gret corage.
```

(225-36)

The summoner and detractors enjoy their own cleverness too much to consider that the potion worked. When at last they conclude that Joseph "With hyre of synne . . . dedyst never muse" (252), they direct their crude accusations toward Mary, whose sin is considered even more base if her betrothed is not the father of the child.

Mary's willingness to drink the potion signals that a quick defeat of the accusers is at hand. The playwright allows them one more chance to prove the depth of their ignorance, however, for they choose to misinterpret her eagerness as a blasphemous challenge of God:

```
Se þis bold bysmare wolde presume
Ageyn god to preve his myght
þow goddys vengeauns hyre xuld consume
Sche wyl not telle hyre fals delyght
þou art with chylde we se in syght

to us þi wombe þe doth accuse
þer was nevyr woman ȝitt in such plyght
þat ffrom mankynde hyre kowde excuse.
```

(265-72)

The detractors find in the word "excuse" a perfect opportunity to allude to the _fabliau_ of the "snow baby," who was conceived when "a flake þer of in to hyre mowthe crepte" (275) and who will melt as soon as the sun shines.[37] Such an allusion is based, once again, on the detractors' willful disregard for the explanation that Mary offers. While the joke itself is enjoyable, the dramatic situation is intensified because the accusers expose their limited vision with such self-assurance.

When these antagonists are finally humiliated in their realization that the couple was telling the truth, the conclusion becomes a scene of repentance and joy. The play thus prepares the spectators to witness the _Birth of Christ_, which follows, with a renewed sense of power in the miracle.

The Chester cycle, too, approaches the mystery and wonder of the Incarnation by emphasizing events that most people would not consider central to the story. In the tightly structured _Wrightes Play_ of the Nativity, the dramatist develops the theme of earthly reality (based on appearances) versus Reality (which is much more difficult to perceive).

Following the resolution of Joseph's doubts in this play, the action moves immediately to an examination of earthly power. Joseph exits by declaring his servitude to God: "Lord God, most of might, / with weale I worshipp thee" (175-76), but this assertion of God's might is at once contrasted with the boasting of Octavian. The flaunting of his stature and his power is comic, especially in light of the greater king who is to be born soon:

138

```
Kinge, coysell, clarke, or knight,
saudens, senatoures in sight,
princes, pryest here nowe dight
and present in this place,
peace! Or here my truthe I plight--
I am the manfulst man of might--
takes mynde on my manece.

All leedes in land bee at my likinge:
castle, conquerour, and kinge
bayne be to doe my byddinge;
yt will non other bee.
Right as I thinke, soe must all bee;
for all the world dose my willinge
and bayne bine when I bydd bringe
homage and feoaltye.
```

(218-32)

The references to medieval titles and institutions indicate that Octavian, instead of engaging in a self-satisfying monologue, is addressing the English spectators and directing their attention to the worldly trappings of power. Based on appearances, the speaker is a mighty ruler; in the context of Christ's birth, however, such symbols of authority are greatly diminished.

The source of humor in such passages is the overriding dramatic irony. Octavian proclaims that "all this world shall witt that wee / bine soveraygne of them all" (271-72), but the audience knows that just the opposite effect will result. Although Octavian admits that mortality limits his power, he does so only to justify the tax he imposes and to stress his own distance from God:

```
For of all flesh, blood, and bonne
made I am, borne of a womane;
and sycker other matter nonne
sheweth not right in mee.
Neyther of iron, tree, ne stonne
am I not wrought, you wott eychone.
And of my life moste parte is gone,
age shewes him soe in mee.

And godhead askes in all thinge
```

139

    tyme that hath noe begininge
    ne never shall have endinge;
    and none of this have I.

                                 (321-32)

Ironically, the tax that is intended to prove that Octavian "hase soverayntee / fullye of all mankynd" (387-88) marks the first of a chain of events--culminating in the trip to Bethlehem and Christ's birth--which shows just the opposite to be true. In spite of such obvious errors in judgment, Octavian is neither offensive nor vapid; rather, he is well developed as a character, especially in his gradual realization that "this childe is more worthye / then such a thowsande as am I" (663-64). As Travis notes, Octavian's "failings make him more human but not more sinful" than other earthly rulers, such as Herod, who are depicted in the plays.[38] His humorous boasting leads to simple piety, as he directs everyone in his empire to worship Christ "with full harte" (688).

Less subtle in its humorous appeal to the audience is the Salome-Tebell(Zelome)[39] incident, also included in the N-Town play of the Nativity. By including the midwives at such a critical moment of biblical history, the playwrights confront the mystery of the Incarnation at its most physical level. In the N-Town version, Mary invites the examination which will prove the miracle to the dubious midwives: "I am clene mayde and pure virgyn / tast with ₃our hand ₃our-self a-lon" (223-24). Only after Zelome confirms that Mary is "modyr nott hurte of virgynite" (232) does the doubt of the second midwife become lewd. Salome asserts,

    I xal nevyr trowe it but I it preve

140

> With hand towchynge but I Assay
> in my conscience it may nevyr cleue
> þat sche hath chylde and is a may.
>
> (245-48)

Mary meets this challenge, too, with an offer for the midwife to "wysely ransake and trye þe trewthe owth" (251). Salome's hand withers, however, and she at last believes this evidence of a miracle.

The more concise Chester version is developed according to the theme of appearance and reality that pervades that play. Instead of touching Mary, Tebell believes in the miracle when she realizes that "shee hath borne a chyld with blys" (531). As in the N-Town play, Salome is more tenacious in her disbelief. Here, however, it is Salome, not Mary, who suggests the idea of confirming physical evidence of virginity, and the fact that she would even imagine such an examination is as obscene as actually carrying it out.

Considering Mary's virginity in such clinical terms is shocking, especially when one tries to imagine tactful staging of such scenes. Although some critics find these interludes distasteful and unnecessary,[40]--and, surely, they do not represent the height of dramatic achievement in the Nativity plays-- they do serve an important dramatic and thematic function.[41] This crude confrontation with Divine Incarnation forces the spectators to see the ridiculousness of Salome's--and their own- -use of earthly measurements to verify miracles. The laughter at the explicit portrayal of the midwife's mistake is thus a final dismissal of the usual earthly perspective. Both plays

141

close with presentations of evidence more powerful than scientific proof: Salome's hand is cured through the intercession of the infant.

Less stylized and more dramatic are the Chester _Adoration_ and the Towneley _Prima Pastorum_ and _Secunda Pastorum_. In each play, the dramatist invents comic action which appears to move away from the central issue, but which instead leads directly to a discussion of the meaning of Divine Incarnation, particularly the patristic interpretation of the Nativity in strongly Eucharistic terms.[42] It is the playwrights' well developed comic emotion that later becomes the source of heartfelt devotion. Such developments of the shepherds' plays differ significantly from the York, true-Coventry, and N-Town versions. After the dramatic climax of Christ's birth, those cycles move to the pastures outside Bethlehem only to have the pious shepherds repeat the prophecies, wonder at the star, and offer their humble, symbolic gifts to the infant.[43] The Chester dramatist and Wakefield Master, however, create shepherds whose dramatic function is much more complex: they are rounded characters whose own stories show the human and personal implications of the Divine Incarnation.

The comic forces at work in these shepherds' plays are effective means of defining those personal implications. Here, as elsewhere in the clusters of plays on the Nativity, comedy is effective to the extent that it takes risks. Its unconventionality suggests a challenge to the traditional view of the Nativity at the same time that it involves the audience in playful dramatic defiance.

One source of comedy in the plays is the dramatists' choice to focus attention on the rough, common people in whose midst Christ was born.[44] If one measures the importance of a charac- ter solely by the number of lines ascribed to him, then such an emphasis takes considerable risks: the audience, without careful direction from the playwright, may lose sight of the central religious event of the play. One way of minimizing such a risk is to develop these characters only as crude contrasts to the holy family, and, as suggested even in their speech, the shep- herds do stand out as lively common folk. A more difficult and dramatically satisfying development, however, is the play- wright's illustration of the similarities, not the differences, between the Nativity and shepherding scenes. In several in- stances, the more appealing human story even seems to take dramatic precedence over its biblical counterpart, for the biblical events of the Nativity are stylized and frozen, com- pared to the vivid animation of the shepherds' lives. The audience never loses sight of that dramatic and theological reality, however, and all of the central comic action is played out against its religious frame.

Each of these plays begins with the three shepherds' com- plaints about the hardships they face. In these vivid and often poetic speeches, the shepherds become fully human, for they echo the despair which all men sometimes feel. This opening passage of the _Prima Pastorum_, for example, establishes Gyb, the first speaker, as a victim of his mutable world:

Lord, what thay ar weyll / that hens ar past!
ffor thay noght feyll / theym to downe cast.
here is mekyll vnceyll / and long has it last,
Now in hart, now in heyll / now in weytt, now
                in blast,
        Now in care,
Now in comforth agane,
Now is fayre, now is rane,
Now in hart full fane,
        And after full sare.

                                        (1-9)

The dramatic effect is to provide immediately a picture of a
world without hope of redemption. Gyb mistrusts wealth and
power, knowing that "When he syttys in pryde, / When it comys on
assay / is kesten downe wyde" (12-13); yet, he has no hope that
one's fortune can be improved. Such complaints define "a world
at its worst--aged, cruel, full of suffering--in order that a
dramatic (and theological) progress might be made therefrom."[45]
Importantly, however, these complaints are emotionally stirring,
and they set the stage dramatically as well as historically.

    The _Prima Pastorum_ emphasizes the poverty of the shepherds,
but always in terms that the spectators easily recognize from
their own experience. Gyb, having lost all his sheep to dis-
ease, must somehow find in his "purs penneles" (33) enough money
to buy a new flock at the fair. Horne also enters despondently,
as he requests to be saved,

        ffrom all myschefys,
        ffrom robers and thefys,
        ffrom those mens grefys,
            That oft ar agans vs.

                                        (51-54)

The comic stanzas that follow, in which Horne criticizes "both
bosters and bragers" (55), would strike familiar chords in the
minds of the spectators. And although the play elicits sympathy

for the shepherds, the tone is often comic. Their use of proverbs to epitomize their hard lot, for example, becomes a contest
to demonstrate whose misery is the most wretched:

> primus pastor. I am euer elyke / wote I neuer
>   what it gars,
> Is none in this ryke / a shepard farys wars.
>   ijus pastor. poore men ar in the dyke / and
>   oft tyme mars,
> The warld is slyke / also helpars
>   Is none here.
> primus pastor. It is sayde full ryfe,
> "a man may not wyfe
> And also thryfe,
>   And all in a yere."
>
>   ijus pastor. ffyrst must vs crepe / and
>   sythen go.
>
>   (91-100)

Gyb's pretending that he already has his sheep is also
comic, for instead of enjoying the wealth he imagines, he argues
with Horne about where the herd should graze. They direct the
invisible sheep in different directions, threatening one another
for control of the animals:

>   ijus pastor. I say, tyr!
> primus pastor. I say, tyr, now agane!
> I say skyp ouer the plane.
>   ijus pastor. wold thou neuer so fane,
>   Tup, I say, whyr!
>
> primus pastor. What, wyll thou not yit / I say,
>   let the shepe go?
> Whop!
>   Secundus pastor. abyde yit. /
> primus pastor.   Will thou bot so?
> knafe, hens I byd flytt / as good that thou do,
> Or I shall the hytt / on thi pate, lo,
>   shall thou reyll;
> I say, gyf the shepe space.
>
>   (113-23)

One can imagine the response to such a scene: the humor of
watching two men fight about nothing is intensified by the

145

spectators' memories of "invisible sheep" they see others arguing about in their own lives. The laughter here, as in much of the Wakefield Master's canon, is not an end in itself, for the source of the joke--the difference between visible and invisible, appearance and reality--is also an important theme of the play. One critic, while not denying the "hilarity of the action," finds the spiritual implication to be strong:

> When the shepherds shout at imaginary sheep as though they were real, they invest what is invisible with substance and reality, and in so doing, show themselves receptive to the possibility of a miracle.[46]

This serious reading does not, however, override the humor of the scene, and the enjoyment of the game is not suddenly exchanged for spiritual symbolism.

The appearance of Slow-pace, who considers himself the most prudent of the shepherds, could end the comic development by demonstrating the folly of the others' disagreement. This wise shepherd, however, ironically proves himself to be as foolish as the others.[47] Although he criticizes the uselessness of their effort, Slow-pace wastes an entire sack of grain simply to make a point. If this action were mimed,[48] then Slow-pace is doubly foolish: "he would then appear to accept the existence of what is invisible as a stage convention while rejecting it as a religious doctrine."[49] The spectators recognize in him, too, a person they know well.

The opening of the <u>Secunda Pastorum</u> reveals a similar comic emphasis in its treatment of the shepherds. This play, too, begins on a serious note, as the first shepherd laments his having to endure such bitter weather. Although his miserable situation is likely to evoke sympathy, the Wakefield Master quickly shifts tones. The complaint of the second shepherd consists of comic exaggeration of the woes of wedded men. Daw, the third shepherd, is presented as equally comic; for, in his protest of the way servants are treated, he immediately reduces the general lament to a personal grievance against his master. And the defiance with which he says, "'lyght chepe / letherly for-yeldys'" (170-71) is humorously overstated, since Daw would be much less rebellious were his master able to hear him.

The Chester _Adoration_ devotes similar attention to the characterization of the shepherds. Especially after the stylized closing of the Nativity play which precedes it, the opening speech is vivid in its presentation of Hankeyn, the first shepherd. Like the Towneley shepherds, Hankeyn takes an unusual pride in his hardship, for he enumerates those diseases he has had to purge from his flock:

> For with walkynge werye I have mee rought;
> besydes the suche my sheepe I sought.
> My taytfull tuppes are in my thought,
> them to save and heale
> from the shrewde scabbe yt sought,
> or the rotte, yf yt were wrought.
> If the cough had them caught
> of hyt I could them heale.
>
> (9-16)

Such boasting is amusing, first of all, in that it is a deliberately "comic exploration of the obsessive way in which simple men talk about the thing they know best."[50] This humor is intensified by the sheer extensiveness of the list and the fact that the other shepherds elaborate on the same subject.

Thus, the opening speeches establish not only a lively and interesting pace for the play, but a dramatic foundation as well.[51] As Kolve points out, this beginning also sets forth an important theme for a Nativity play: the arrival of Christ, the healer, in the sacrament of Eucharist.[52] The theme is not defined clearly at this point in the play, but the metaphor is strongly suggested--even in the fact that these catalogues of ailments immediately follow the presentation of Christ's birth. The result is that the plays are simultaneously serious and playful, for the miraculous birth has not changed the poverty and oppression of the shepherds. Although the characters themselves are unaware of the insolence suggested in their complaints, the plays comically impose questions about Christ as a healer--questions which are resolved only when the spectators witness the limitation of human perception as it is so delightfully portrayed in the shepherds' base imitation of angelic singing.

The shepherds' unconscious use of anachronisms is another important source of dramatic and comic strength and a means of continuing to focus the play on human understanding of the Incarnation. Although such references are typical of Middle English literature, the frequency with which anachronisms appear in both of the Towneley plays, in particular, points to a greater purpose than eliciting an occasional laugh. Some of these anachronisms are blurted out as simple oaths, and although the use of Christ's name is historically impossible, the sense of the speech is consistent with the tone the shepherds usually

148

adopt. Examples are the first shepherd's statement in Secunda Pastorum, "That is right, by the roode! / thyse nyghtys ar long" (182), and Tudd's request in Chester, "Trowle, boy, for Godes tree, / come eate a morsell with me" (226-27). Because these anachronisms are logically placed in the speeches, they draw little attention to themselves.

More noticeable and dramtically useful are those explicit reminders of events in Christ's life. In the Secunda Pastorum, the second shepherd's complaint about his wife specifically mentions "Hyr pater noster" (104) and "hym that dyed for vs all" (107). The night spells offered by Slow-pace and Mak echo phrases that the shepherds could not have known and that the audience could not have missed:

> iijus pastor. ffor ferde we be fryght / a
>   crosse lett vs kest,
> Cryst crosse, benedyght / eest and west,
>   ffor drede.
> Ihesus, onazorus,
> Crucyefixus,
> Morcus, andreus,
>   God be oure spede!
>   (Prima Pastorum, 289-95)

> Mak. Then myght I lett you bedene / of that
>   ye wold rowne,
>   No drede.
> ffro my top to my too,
> Manus tuas commendo,
> poncio pilato,
>   Cryst crosse me spede!
>   (Secunda Pastorum, 263-68)

The dramatic situation becomes more complex, for, clearly, traditional historical time is not at work here. And in the ironic humor of the shepherds' references is a serious reminder of the miracle which occurred to save, not curse, mankind. The value of the Crucifixion as well as the Divine Incarnation, is impudently challenged in the tone of these night spells, for Mak invokes the power of "Cryst crosse" with an underlying indication that black magic is at work. Dramatically, the effect of this scene is to intensify interest in Mak--who, in spite of this cavorting, does succeed in casting a spell on the shepherds--and in the theological question suggested in his strange anachronisms.

The playwrights also use many secular anachronisms, allusions which put medieval English traditions and expressions in the mouths of the shepherds. Whereas the religious anachronisms are comic in their irony and their ability to surprise the audience, the English developments are like favorite jokes. They encourage the spectators to participate in the shepherds' story and to view the pastoral world as one not unlike the English countryside. Descriptions of clothing and food are medieval, not biblical, and the shepherds use homey proverbs to illustrate their points. Even the names given in the texts-- Gyb, John Horne, Slow-pace, Daw, Trowle, Tudd, Hankeyn, Harvye-- suggest contemporaneity. The Chester play is laden with specific references when, for example, the second shepherd describes some of his food: "butter that bought was in Blakon" (115), "ale of Halton" (117), and "a jannock of Lancastershyre" (120).

Such references are humorous in their impossibility, but they also present great risks for the dramatists. Much more direct than the religious anachronisms, these secular references which establish medieval England as the setting for Advent taunt the spectators with an unsettling thought: if poverty, oppression, and sorrow still exist centuries after Christ's life on earth, then perhaps the Incarnation did not actually redeem mankind.[53] No rational debate on this subject appears in the plays, nor is this suggestion developed explicitly at any point. The spectators are nevertheless drawn to participate emotionally in the dramatist's toying with the idea that the basis of their faith may have been the successful disguising of another sheep-child.

The Wakefield and Chester dramatists rely on parody as a means of playfully agitating and then resolving doubts. A more sophisticated humor than the simple lewd remark or punning wordplay, parody depends for its success on the spectators' understanding the whole picture. A play which essentially focuses on the Nativity is well suited for such a development, since the members of the audience are quite familiar with the story of Christ's birth. Parody, however, is particularly risky in the religious context: the dramatist must find a balance between mocking his subject matter and elevating it through coarse imitation.

The most famous parody is the sheep-stealing incident which comprises much of the action in the Secunda Pastorum. The entire Mak episode emphasizes the childbirth theme which is central to the play; more importantly, however, the inclusion of this sheep-stealer is a decidedly earthly parody of the divine Nativity. For Mak, the birth of a child is an economic burden, not a source of joy. In his opening address, Mak wishes he

151

"were in heuen / for there wepe no barnes" (194), and, when
discovered by the shepherds, he expresses fully the suffering
his wife and children cause:

> Mak. lyys walteryng, by the roode / by the
>   fyere, lo!
> And a howse full of brude / she drynkys well to;
> yll spede othere good / that she wyll do!
>   Bot so
> Etys as fast as she can,
> And ilk yere that commys to man
> She bryngys furth a lakan,
>   And som yeres two.
>
> (236-43)

In this clever evasion of the charges that he "has an yll noys /
of stelyng of shepe" (225), Mak also begins to establish evidence that he will need once he has stolen a sheep. Such an
impassioned speech, however, goes beyond the function of plot:
in his exaggerated humility, in his wonder at the fertility of
his wife, and in his debasement at the hands of "a fowll dowse"
(246), the audience hears echoes of Joseph's own complaints
against Mary.[54]

Although a legend of a sheep or hog disguised as an infant
was an important source for the play,[55] the playwright adapts
the tradition to reinforce the parallels between the sacred
birth and its base counterpart. On a dramatic level, Mak's
allusion to the newborn child in his dream--a child which the
audience knows to be a sheep--is a reminder that the best part
of the joke is yet to come. And Mak unintentionally endows his
speech with obvious and appropriate symbolism for a Nativity
play: he speaks of the birth of "a yong lad, / ffor to mend oure
flok" (388). The iconography of the Lamb of God is elicited in

such a remark, even though Mak, himself, is speaking sarcastically about the sheep-child.[56]

The parody of the Nativity, suggested first in Gyll's "unnatural" propagation, continues on a symbolic level. In its most simple terms, the lamb Mak steals is made human in his game, so that the couple can escape punishment and enjoy the meal they "lyst well ete" (323). The unmistakable parallels between this story and the Divine Incarnation are drawn consistently in the play, ultimately embedding in the coarse stage humor a comic re-examination of the mystical birth. These close parallels serve a greater purpose than ensuring that the spectators recognize and enjoy the parody of Divine Incarnation; they force the audience to see concurrently both earthly and divine perspectives. Although it is a precarious position, the playwright intensifies his portrait of the miracle by temporarily casting off the traditional nimbuses from the heads of Christ and his earthly parents--a transformation accomplished through Mak's reminders of the burdens of adding yet another child and through Gyll's enactment of the physical pain of childbirth. Before the spectators are invited to celebrate with awe the mystery of Christ's divinity, the playwright imposes this vivid, even startling, presentation of the miracle of Christ's humanity.

One source of humor is Mak's complex role in the parody. Although critics debate whether Mak should be viewed as Antichrist[57]--thus completing the inversion of the Nativity--there are sufficient references in the text to suggest that he is

153

something other than human: his disguise, sleeping spell, strange curse, and frequent references to the devil. Just as the anachronistic references warp the sense of time in the play, the deliberately ambiguous characterization of Mak confuses his role in the historical narrative. The mystery associated with Mak prepares the audience to anticipate not only the birth of the sheep-child, but also the divine birth it parodies.[58] The best part of this important characterization, however, is that Mak is never presented in a traditionally didactic way. Even when he "steals the Lamb of God Who takes away the sins of the world and Who grants us mercy and peace,"[59] Mak functions as much more than a symbolic character. He remains dramatically rounded in his humorous attempts to conceal his theft.

The most well-developed joke in the play centers on Mak as the putative father of the "child" in the cradle. Once the shepherds have searched Mak's home but "can fynde no flesh" (544), Mak decides to play with them a bit. Although he and Gyll behave as if a child has been born, they and the spectators never forget that it is the stolen sheep which lies swaddled beside them. This knowledge lets the audience in on the obscene implication of Mak's comment: "Any lord myght hym haue / This chyld to his son" (556). A purely symbolic reading of this line misses the point of its humor. For example, in her analysis of the sophisticated implication of the word knaue, Linda Marshall assumes that very subtle irony--not a hilarious joke--is the intention:

> . . . there is play with the words "lord" and
> "son" as persons of the Trinity, since the lamb

> in the cradle, if typologically he is Antichrist
> and his ministry, is indeed the offspring of
> "any" lord, any earthly master in league with
> Satan.[60]

The dramatic irony of the crude allusion is that the shepherds miss its full meaning; but it is also ironic because it is such a base reduction of the "unnatural" conception of Christ. Since the audience knows that Mak is playing, the surprise of the audacious implied parallel is enjoyable.

When the shepherds return to give a sixpence to the child, the issue of paternity continues, but here the joke is on Mak. Recognizing their lost sheep in the cradle, the shepherds make Mak squirm as they comically point out the child's unusual features: "he has a long snowte" (585); "he is merkyd amys" (586); and "he is lyke to oure shepe!" (589). Daw, the third shepherd, acknowledges that they are victims of a "hee frawde" (594), and makes this tongue-in-cheek remark about the child: "Sagh I neuer in a credyll / A hornyd lad or now" (600-01).[61]

Even more humorous are the couple's outrageous attempts to continue the game. Mak announces, "I am he that hym gatt / and yond woman hym bare" (603), and he and Gyll desperately try to explain the misshapen child:

> iijus pastor. I know hym by the eere marke /
>   that is a good tokyn.
> Mak. I tell you, syrs, hark! / hys noyse was
>   brokyn.
> Sythen told me a clerk / that he was forspokyn.
> primus pastor. This is a fals wark / I wold
>   fayn be wrokyn:
> Gett wepyn.
> Vxor. he was takyn with an elfe,
> I saw it myself.
> when the clok stroke twelf
>   was he forshapyn.
>
> (611-19)

As one might expect, these explanations fail, and Mak is tossed in a blanket as mild punishment.[62] Although the nature of the comedy differs significantly from the treatment of Joseph as a cuckolded husband, the effect on the audience is similar. The situation is dramatically compelling and encourages animated delivery, but it is also thematically appealing. The dramatist plays with the idea that the sheep-child, like Christ, was conceived through deception, even magic. Such a suggestion does not encourage the spectators to forget that this is a domestic low comedy and that a greater reality lies behind it all; however, this effective use of parody temporarily blurs the distinctions between earthly and spiritual perceptions of the event.

Gyll's equivocal oath works in a similar way. As the shepherds search the house, she pledges her innocence by promising something that she would be glad to uphold:

> A, my medyll!
> I pray to god so mylde,
> If euer I you begyld,
> That I ete this chylde
> That lygys in this credyll.
>
> (534-38)

An important characteristic of the legends on which this story was based,[63] the oath functions here as more than a source of ironic humor. In a Corpus Christi play about the Nativity, the symbol of the Eucharist is also implied. The Wakefield Master inserts this doctrine so subtly that the play does not shift to a purely symbolic representation. Instead, the deftly placed allusions to the real subject matter accrue until the scene shifts to the stable in Bethlehem.

The Towneley _Prima Pastorum_ and Chester _Adoration_ develop more fully the parody of the Eucharist. As the shepherds meet to share an elaborate feast, their actions and speeches suggest a clear parallel to the events of the Mass. Thus, the dramatists, playing with the idea of Divine Incarnation as it is re-enacted in consecration and communion, invite the spectators to examine comically the meaning of the Nativity as an everyday event.

Echoing the consecration and other parts of the Mass, the Chester shepherds invite God to "come eate with us" (139), and the third shepherd makes this double-edged remark about the wine they drink: "Such lickour makes men to live; / this game may noewhere be leste" (147-48). Similar references to the events of the Mass are played out in the _Prima Pastorum_, such as in the third shepherd's reference to the kiss of peace: "By my thryft we must kys" (263). As critics have recognized, however, the meal that they share is imaginary.[64] They unpack the assortment of meats not with stage properties or even with the kind of mime which asks the spectators to perceive the food as theatrically real. Instead, they invent the meal to satisfy their hunger, creating "a restorete / To make a good appete" (238-39). Gyb's qualifications of the list--"I wene," "I trow"--suggest that he is inventing the dishes as he goes, becoming involved in the imaginative game they have established.

Interestingly, although the meal is illusory, its ability to regenerate the hungry shepherds is real. As they drink the

157

imagined wine or ale--they never resolve which--the shepherds
seem to forget the troubles they had bemoaned earlier:

<u>primus pastor</u>. yee speke all by clerge[te],
 I here by your clause;
Cowth ye by youre gramery / reche vs a drynk,
I shuld be more mery / ye wote What I thynk.
 <u>ijus pastor</u>. haue good ayll of hely / bewar
 now, I wynk,
ffor and thou drynk drely / in thy poll wyll
 it synk.
 <u>primus pastor</u>. A, so;
This is boyte of oure bayll,
good holsom ayll.
 <u>iijus pastor</u>. ye hold long the skayll,
 Now lett me go to.

           (240-50)

On a comic level, the scene offers several opportunities to
laugh at the shepherds as they argue, for example, about who has
drunk the most. Although Cawley finds the source of humor here
to be the "incongruity [achieved] by mixing together aristo-
cratic and plebian dishes,"[65] Kolve's assessment of the humor is
more likely:

> Surely the humor lies in the sheer size of the
> meal: what in the Coventry cycle and the French
> plays is a kind of medieval box lunch is here a
> gargantuan banquet. And there is further laugh-
> ter in the way in which the shepherds produce the
> feast, like conjurers, pulling out this and that
> from all corners of their clothing. Medieval
> feasts were known for their lavishness, but this
> is a meal for only three men, and it is served in
> the fields out of pockets and packets. The
> manner of its making and its disproportionate
> size constitute the comedy of <u>both</u> [the Chester
> and <u>Prima Pastorum</u>] versions.[66]

Seeing the shepherds as "conjurers" is a useful perception, one
which depends on and develops the parody of the Incarnation.
The shepherds use "gramery" to invoke the redemptive powers of
imagined food and drink, and through this ritual are enough

removed from the cares of their world to be satisfied. The discrepancies between this parody and its obvious parallel to the sacrament of Eucharist are comic and surprising: the feast of unleavened bread is turned into an elaborate secular meal, and the sacrificial wine becomes the spirit powerful enough to take a man's breath away.

Especially in a play that leads, ultimately, to the Nativity, part of the comic effect lies in the surprise at the greater underlying parallel. In making a joke of the "gramery" which presumably transforms air into a lavish banquet, the playwright treads dangerous ground, for he toys with the doctrine of transubstantiation and the sacrament which makes Christ's coming a contemporary event: "in the Mass, the wine is turned into blood through the medium of the Priest's learning (gramere), and through his good magic (gramerye)."[67] This ambiguity, although risky, is necessary for the play to succeed on an emotional level. The involvement demanded by the stage action does not allow the audience to remove itself from the struggle between conflicting perspectives. Thus the Wakefield Master presents his audience with a different form of the same question suggested in the play's opening: is Christ's presence invented, like the shepherds' meal, to satisfy spiritual hunger, or does the Incarnation actually exist in the daily lives of average people?

Unlike the plays of Cain and Abel or Joseph's Doubts, here there is no rational confrontation between absolute faith and critical disbelief. The question is suggested entirely through parody and articulated only in the secular antics of the shepherds. The spectators, instead of being lured to consider such a question rationally, are encouraged to participate in the game, to play with doubt without ever having to relinquish their belief. The audience thus looks to the closing Nativity scene with the same knowledge of earthly limitations and hope in divine miracle as the shepherds.

In each of the cycles, the game reaches its turning point when the shepherds hear the proclamation of Christ's birth. The Chester Adoration and the Secunda Pastorum, in particular, use this angelic song as the emotional hinge on which the dramatic success hangs. When the shepherds are brought to a direct confrontation with a miracle, their musical parody serves to focus the blur of earthly and spiritual perceptions, leaving a clear image of what is Real and what is illusory. And their limited perception--as they argue about the Latin phrases and croak presumably horrible renditions of the song--becomes laughable in its insistence on understanding the grammar of the message before sensing its enormous implication. The Chester and Towneley playwrights, in particular, use this parody of the angel's song to encourage continued emotional intensity as the spectators perceive the Nativity and its symbolic counterparts.

The Secunda Pastorum uses the song as a link between the conclusion of the Mak episode and the beginning of a traditional Nativity scene. In a typical demonstration of their limited perception, these shepherds react to an announcement of the Savior's birth by analyzing the song's delivery instead of its overwhelming message:

<u>primus pastor</u>. This was a qwant stevyn /
    that euer yit I hard.
It is a meruell to neuyn / thus to be skard.

. . .

<u>ijus pastor</u>. Say, what was his song? /
    hard ye not how he crakyd it?
Thre brefes to a long. /
<u>iijus pastor</u>.   yee, mary, he hakt it.
was no crochett wrong / nor no thyng that lakt
    it.
                                        (647-59)

This technical discussion of the song is an amusing reminder
that there are vast differences between the shepherds' perceptions and what actually exists. Their own song, although not
articulated in the text itself, succeeds in building emotion as
it sharpens the sense of mystery. Instead of rational explanations and allusions, the closing of the play relies on this
intensity of emotion as a means of reconciling the paradox of
Divine Incarnation. Through their admittedly feeble imitation,
the shepherds recognize the limitations of the senses in understanding miracle. The joyful close of the play dispels doubt
and affirms the spectators' awe in the miraculous paradoxes of
Christ's birth.

The Chester <u>Adoration</u> expands the shepherds' analysis of
the song: more than 75 lines are devoted to their explication of
the "Gloria." Unlike the Towneley shepherds, who approach the
song from a musical perspective, these shepherds try to comprehend the unfamiliar Latin terms:

TERTIUS PASTOR
What song was this, saye yee,
that he sange to us all three?

                                     161

    Expounded shall yt bee
    erre wee hethen passe;
    for I am eldest of degree
    and alsoe best, as seemes mee,
    hit was 'grorus glorus' with a 'glee.'
    Hit was neyther more nor lasse.

                         GARCIUS
    Nay, yt was 'glorus glarus glorius';
    methinke that note went over the howse.
    A seemely man hee was, and curiouse;
    but soone awaye hee was.

                      PRIMUS PASTOR
    Nay, yt was 'glorus glarus' with a 'glo,'
    and mych of 'celsis' was therto.
    As ever have I rest or woo,
    much hee spake of 'glas.'

                                        (376-91)

They eventually understand the spirit, if not the letter, of the
angel's message, for they reveal the effects of this announcement. Harvye states, "I quoked when hee so whewted" (422), and
Trowle, too, is moved: "Hee sange alsoe of a 'Deo'; / me thought
that heled my harte" (430-31). F.M. Salter suggests that "for
breath-taking, colossal impudence the scene is without rival in
drama."[68] Although in some ways the scene is overstated--for
example, in Joseph's detailed explanation of the miracle and in
the ritual of offering the gifts--its effect is breathtaking:
gradually the discord among the shepherds disappears. Even
Trowle is changed, for he is moved to complete repentance at the
sight of the Christ Child:[69]

    Solace nowe to see this
    byldes in my brest blys:
    never after to do amys,
    thinge that him loth ys.

                                        (492-95)

Unlike the "solace" the shepherds found in their meal, the
comfort offered here is neither contrived nor ephemeral. It is

the height of the Corpus Christi feast and a fitting, emotional conclusion to the shepherds' play.

A useful distinction Munson makes regarding the _Prima Pastorum_ is the essential point of several shepherds' plays: "truth has to do with imagination and choice. This applies no less to religious truth than to truth about sheep, grain, or feasts."[70] The frightening possibility proposed through the humor of the Chester dramatist and Wakefield Master is that one may choose to deny miracles or to use limited human perception to question the validity of religious wonder. The shepherds' choice to follow the star, presumably a "dazzlingly visible prop,"[71] marks a return to a stance with which the audience is familiar. The dramatic effect is relief and resolution--even joy--as the spectators, as well as the shepherds, affirm their choice that this miracle is the Reality against which their faith is measured. Comic developments in the plays are instrumental in achieving this end: anachronism, emphasis on low characters, and parody create a synergistic blur of religious and earthly themes. The life infused in the traditional Nativity narration charges it with an energy toward which the audience is drawn. The often boisterous activity on stage is dramatically compelling, demanding more of an emotional than intellectual response to the implicit questions in the plays. Thus the spectators play with one of the most sacred mysteries of the Christian tradition--the miracle of the word becoming flesh and dwelling among men--and through their game arrive at serious, intense conclusions about the importance of the Incarnation as

163

both an historical event and an everyday choice of faith.

Notes

[1] Stanley J. Kahrl, _Traditions of Medieval English Drama_ (1974; rpt. Pittsburgh: University of Pittsburgh Press, 1975), p. 86.

[2] William F. Munson, "Audience and Meaning in Two Medieval Dramatic Realisms," _Comparative Drama_, 9 (1975), 44.

[3] In Matthew 1:19, Joseph's hesitation is mentioned only briefly: "Then Joseph her husband, being a just man, and not willing to make her a publick example, was minded to put her away privily." For a survey of treatments in the plays, see Philip Cormac Deasy, _St. Joseph in the English Mystery Plays_ (Washington, D.C.: Catholic University Press, 1937). See also Prosser, pp. 89-102.

[4] Woolf, p. 169. Woolf studies the Joseph plays in light of their sources, pp. 163-79, arguing that both religious and secular influences shaped the depiction of Joseph and his dilemma in the mystery cycles.

[5] Woolf asserts that "in accordance with these satiric or burlesque traditions, Joseph sees himself in the contemptible role of an old man, feeble and impotent, married to a wanton young wife who has taken an equally young lover in his place," p. 170. See also Meyer Schapiro, "'Muscipula Diaboli': The Symbolism of the Merode Altarpiece," _Art Bulletin_, 27 (1945), 184; Schapiro explains that this liberty in characterization was possible because the cult of Joseph was entirely undeveloped at the end of the fourteenth century: the feast of Joseph "did not enter the Roman breviary until 1479 and became obligatory for the entire Church only in 1621." See also Gail McMurray Gibson, "'Porta haec clausa erit': Comedy, Conception, and Ezekiel's Closed Door in the _Ludus Coventriae_ Play of 'Joseph's Return,'" _Journal of Medieval and Renaissance Studies_, 8 (1978), 139-40.

[6] Prosser, arguing that such a quick resolution fails dramatically, criticizes the Chester treatment of Joseph. In her view, because the scene of Joseph's doubt does not include a dialogue with Mary, it functions solely as a brief interlude, p. 90. Peter W. Travis agrees with Prosser's charge that the play lacks conflict, but he states that "this is precisely its intent; unlike the tragic rite of passage projected in the Chester 'Passion,' for example, the ceremonial transitions of the 'Nativity' are achieved with a minimum of anxiety and an absence of guilt." In _Dramatic Design in the Chester Cycle_ (Chicago: The University of Chicago Press, 1982), p. 116.

[7] Joseph L. Baird and Lorrayne Y. Baird, citing similar references in _Decameron_ and Mirk's _Festial_, explain that stories

164

of boys in angel's clothes "must have been widely spread and well-known, since they ultimately contaminate the Annunciation story itself." In "Fabliau Form and the Hegge Joseph's Return," Chaucer Review, 8 (1973), 169. Woolf points out that this fabliau implication is also developed in Pseudo-Matthew, considered an important source for the treatment of Joseph in the plays. When confronted by Mary's attendant, Joseph responds, "It could be that someone disguised himself as an angel of the Lord and deceived her" [Woolf's translation], p. 170.

[8] Prosser suggests that, unlike the York play from which it was derived, the Towneley play achieves a doctrinal resolution. Joseph repents not only for his angry words, but also for his sin of doubt, pp. 93-95.

[9] Prosser's main point is that the structure in Towneley avoids the double-rise one sees in the action of the York play, where Joseph leaves twice and confronts Mary twice. The result is "a plot of progressing action, of increasing tension," p. 93.

[10] Prosser, p. 96.

[11] Theresa Coletti, in an article which outlines the evidence of Marian iconography in the N-Town cycle, notes that this attention to Mary's life before the birth of Christ is unique, for it shows "extraordinary consciousness of the motifs and interpretations that characterized late medieval devotion to the Virgin." In "Devotional Iconography in the N-Town Marian Plays," Comparative Drama, 11 (1977), 22. See also Fry, pp. 544-51; and Woolf, pp. 160-61.

[12] See also the Chester Nativity, 11. 27-40; and York Annunciation, 11. 177-84.

[13] Coletti finds the symbolism to be consistent with late medieval pictorial representations, many of which are based on "the popular metaphor that compared the event to sunlight passing through glass," pp. 29-30.

[14] This view of Mary as the second Eve was a popular medieval tradition, including the Ave-Eva wordplay one sees, for example, in this thirteenth-century lyric:
All this world was forlore
Eva peccatrice,
Till our lord was ibore
De te genitrice.
With 'Ave' it went away,
Thuster night, and cometh the day
Salutis.
The welle springeth ut of thee
Virtutis.
In R.T. Davies, Medieval English Lyrics (Evanston, Illinois: Northwestern University Press, 1964), p. 53. Woolf notes that the Protevangelium extends this relationship to include Joseph:

165

in that apocryphal gospel, Joseph remarks that Eve's deception is repeated and that Adam's fate is now his, pp. 171-72. Within the cycle plays, reference to this tradition is also evident in the Towneley prologue to Annunciation:

> Angell must to mary go,
> ffor the feynd was eue fo;
> he was foule and layth to syght,
> And thou art angell fayr and bright.
>
> (61-64)

[15] Woolf, p. 172.

[16] Baird and Baird, referring to two distinct allusions to fabliaux in this cycle, state that "this playwright is unique among the dramatists in his interest in, and exploitation of . . . the fabliau," p. 160.

[17] Baird and Baird, p. 161.

[18] Coletti remarks that "from the beginnings of Christian theology light had supplied a metaphor for religious mysteries" and had often been characteristic of pictorial representations of Mary, p. 29.

[19] Baird and Baird cite several examples of this blindness as it appears in the fabliaux and in Chaucer's Merchant's Tale, p. 162. They also note that "the contemptible figure of the blind, impotent old man is a perfect externalization of his spiritual darkness," p. 168.

[20] See Baird and Baird, pp. 163-64, for an explanation of the stratagems used by wives in the cuckolded husband tradition.

[21] See, for example, the true-Coventry Shearmen and Taylors' Pageant, ll. 133-35, and Towneley Annunciation, ll. 302-05.

[22] Prosser, p. 98.

[23] See Prosser, pp. 99-101, for an explanation of the parallels between this play and Love's Mirrour. An important departure from the source is the N-Town playwright's development of Joseph's anger, for in Mirrour Joseph becomes a model of the patient husband.

[24] The reference to an angelic accomplice is further evidence that Joseph cannot look past his human perception, for the involvement of an accomplice is an important feature in many of the fabliaux. See Baird and Baird, pp. 163-64.

[25] Gibson, p. 144.

[26] Gibson, pp. 150-51.

[27] For example, Baird and Baird point out that emphasis here is on "the gift of divine revelation which makes repentance possible," p. 168. And Gibson states that in the course of the play, "the despairing Joseph will learn to replace his blind prophecy of the Son with certain knowledge of Him," p. 155.

[28] Prosser, p. 102.

[29] Gibson, too, avoids such a discussion. Although she acknowledges that there is humor and indecency in Joseph's Return, her study assumes that the overt religious symbolism was stronger in making a dramatic impact: "The critical issue is not whether bawdiness exists in the plays of Joseph's Doubts, but in what context it exists, not whether humor is evoked, but how it is ultimately resolved," pp. 138-39.

[30] Baird and Baird, p. 164.

[31] See Prosser, pp. 90-101, for a comparison of dramatic unity in the plays.

[32] Prosser notes that this rapid repentance is "wholly unrealistic to the modern mind. Few today believe that a man can change in one brief moment," pp. 101-02. In her assessment, this complete transformation is the source of the mystery, one that cannot be explained. Even for the medieval audience, however, the speed with which the stubborn old man relents is so remarkable as to be comic.

[33] Using Mankind as the starting point for his discussion of medieval comedy, W.A. Davenport describes this structure as the basis of the exemplum-play. In the Towneley Secunda Pastorum and the N-Town Trial of Joseph and Mary, however, he maintains that the didactic feature is absorbed into the dramatic situation: "the basic three-part structure of moral introduction, exemplary narrative and resolution in Christian hope and love is visible, but the relationship of the parts is oblique, not explicit." In Fifteenth-century English Drama: The Early Moral Plays and their Literary Relations (Cambridge: D.S. Brewer, 1982), pp. 55-60. Watt notes that "such a formula has the flavor of the typical Elizabethan comedy--sad, unstable beginning and happy ending," p. 160. See also William W.E. Slights, "The Incarnations of Comedy," University of Toronto Quarterly, 51 (1981), 19-20.

[34] Woolf observes that while hints of comic themes appear in this cycle, the York dramatist concerns himself primarily with presenting "the dignity of simple virtue," p. 183.

[35] Davenport, p. 59.

[36] Davenport explains that the play is based on "the Apocryphal story that Mary and Joseph had taken vows of virginity, and, when Mary was known to be pregnant, were tried, Joseph for

167

breaking his vow and Mary for adultery, and required to prove their innocence by drinking a bitter draught, the drink of vengeance, which would disfigure or harm them if guilty. The story was told by Lydgate in his Life of our Lady and this . . . is the probable source of the dramatist's interest in the subject," p. 57. See also Woolf, pp. 174-77.

[37] Baird and Baird, pp. 160-61.

[38] Travis, p. 115.

[39] Hardin Craig accounts for the differences in name by alluding to the French background which is usually assumed for the Chester cycle. Le Mistere du Viel Testament is considered an important source for this cycle, and--as Craig notes--critics support this hypothesis by remarking that "in other English plays and in the apocryphal source the midwives in the Nativity are Salome and Zelumi, whereas in Chester and in the French plays they are Salome and Zebel or Tebel," p. 176.

[40] Travis, for example, finds "Salome's expression of incomprehension . . . too shocking to summon much fellow feeling," p. 115. Woolf, discussing the N-Town play, bases her repugnance partly on a possible "prudish reaction" to such a scene, but more importantly on the basis of methodology: "the method of the apocryphal gospels, which is to discredit incredulity by a proliferation of sensational miracles, seems aesthetically inadequate to the subject-matter," p. 179.

[41] Kevin J. Harty suggests that didactic unity is also achieved through this "proclamation of faith," for "the two midwives attest the fulfillment of the prophecy of the virgin birth in Isaiah 7:14, previously recited to the audience in Chester Play V." In "'Unbeleeffe Is a Fowle Sinne': The Chester Nativity Play," Susquehanna University Studies, 11 (1979), 39.

[42] See Leah Sinanoglou, "The Christ Child as Sacrifice: A Medieval Tradition and the Corpus Christi Plays,: Speculum, 48 (1973), 494 ff. Sinanoglou bases her study on the theory that Gregory's symbolic reading of the Nativity story became "a medieval commonplace, repeated in England as early as the homilies of Aelfric and reflected in the frequency with which art and literature paired wheat and the Christ Child." This motif is implied to some extent in all of the cycles, Sinanoglou suggests, but becomes central to the themes of the Towneley plays. See also Coletti, pp. 31-37, for a discussion of medieval pictorial representations of the Nativity; several of these --such as the ritualistic portrayal of the manger as an altar, or the bread basket hanging over the Christ Child--suggest clear sacramental references which readily translate into stage iconography.

[43] Critics have made much of the symbolic gifts offered in each of the cycles. As Munson succinctly asserts, "the several

168

readings agree that in the Second Shepherds' Play the shepherds' gifts, like the gifts of the Magi, symbolize aspects of the three-person God: mortal humanity, sovereignty, divinity," p. 67. See, for example, John P. Cutts, "The Shepherds' Gifts in the Second Shepherds' Play and Bosch's 'Adoration of the Magi'," Comparative Drama, 4 (1970), 120-24; Lawrence J. Ross, "Symbol and Structure in the Secunda Pastorum" (1967; rpt. in Medieval English Drama, Jerome Taylor and Alan H. Nelson, eds. Chicago: University of Chicago Press, 1972), pp. 183-97; and Lynn Remly, "Deus Caritas: The Christian Message of the 'Secunda Pastorum'," Neuphilologische Mitteilungen, 72 (1971), 746-47.

[44] The Chester Adoration also characterizes its shepherds as rough common folk. Yet the Chester dramatist takes fewer risks, for he presents the wrestling match, the discussions of "pastoral" duties only after the Nativity scene has been presented. The Wakefield Master, on the other hand, allows the shepherds to move the action toward Bethlehem, so that the spectators witness the event as through these commoners' eyes. Interestingly, no apocryphal or meditative sources suggest such an approach; see Woolf, pp. 182-83.

[45] Kolve, p. 167.

[46] Suzanne Speyser, "Dramatic Illusion and Sacred Reality in the Towneley Prima Pastorum," Studies in Philology, 78 (1981), 9-10.

[47] Woolf suggests that here the Wakefield Master brings to life a moral from A Hundred Merry Tales: "this tale showeth you that some man taketh upon him to show other men wisdom when he is but a fool himself," p. 189.

[48] Morgan, pp. 679-80.

[49] Speyser, p. 11.

[50] Kolve, p. 152.

[51] See Lorraine Kochanske Stock, "Comedy in the English Mystery Cycles: Three Comic Scenes in the Chester Shepherds' Play," in Versions of Medieval Comedy, Paul G. Ruggiers, ed. (Norman: University of Oklahoma Press, 1977), pp. 225-26.

[52] Kolve notes that other references in the Chester cycle sharpen the playwright's focus on the metaphor of Christ as physician/healer, as presented in this passage from a fifteenth-century treatise on the sacrament: "I aventure me to resceyue þee, swete lord, as a syke man resseyueþ a medcyne. þou art a sooþfaste leche, lord, and soþely I am syke. þer fore I take þee, for to be moad hool þorou þee," pp. 152-55.

[53] Ross states the effect of these anachronisms without considering the implied risks: they "depict the perennial human

condition before the Incarnation," forcing the view of the Incarnation as "an eternally recurrent mystery," p. 209. Taft, accepting that the play is an "artfully constructed mirror of the 15th-century world," considers only the positive response of the audience. They come to understand the need "to rediscover Christ's legacy to mankind: the New Law," p. 133.

[54] The suggestion that doubling of parts may have occurred reinforces such a parallel, particularly if the actor playing the part of Gyll also plays Mary. See Mack, pp. 81-82. Sinanoglou states that parallel staging achieves a similar effect: Mary is placed in the same position as Gyll, the sheep's cradle is the crib of the Christ Child, and "Mak's bawled lullaby [is] balanced by the angelic chorus heralding the birth of Jesus," p. 507. See also Woolf, p. 191.

[55] See Cosbey, pp. 310-17.

[56] Sinanoglou assures us that "all but the dullest of medieval viewers were accustomed to pairing the two [Christ Child and lamb] in their minds," p. 508. Woolf outlines the complexity of such an icon: "the sheep purporting to be a baby anticipates the baby who was symbolically a lamb, but it is also a grotesque fulfilment of the lamb offered by Abel and the sheep offered in place of Isaac," p. 191. See also Slights, p. 17.

[57] William Manly, for example, asserts that Mak's role is as "dramatic counterbalance. He is the comic antithesis to Christ and the Christian way of life, a role which . . . draws upon that periodic, saturnalian spirit of misrule," p. 154. See also Linda Marshall, pp. 720-36. Marshall supports this implication by analyzing Antichrist legends as they appear in Mak's name and his curses. For considerations of Mak as a "folk-practitioner"--but not Antichrist--see Cosbey, p. 314; and Morgan, pp. 685-87.

[58] Mack, p. 81.

[59] Taft, p. 135, suggests that a medieval audience would have immediately made this association.

[60] Linda Marshall, p. 732.

[61] Slights argues that this revelation is an important turning point, for "only the fact of the flesh--the sheep's snout, horns, and earmark, and later God's incarnation--can penetrate the deceptions forged by the human mind and shock sinful man into embracing God's clear truth," p. 17.

[62] For a discussion of the blanket tossing as punishment, see Claude Chidamian, "Mak and the Tossing in the Blanket," Speculum, 22 (1947), 186-90; and Mack, pp. 81-82.

[63] See Cosbey, p. 314.

[64] This theory was first proposed by A.C. Cawley, "The 'Grotesque' Feast in the *Prima Pastorum*," *Speculum*, 30 (1955), 213-17. For discussions of the dramatic and theological advantages of miming the feast, see Speyser, pp. 12-16; and Alicia K. Nitecki, "The Sacred Elements of the Secular Feast in *Prima Pastorum*," *Mediaevalia*, 3 (1977), pp. 229-31.

[65] Cawley, p. 213.

[66] Kolve, pp. 160-61.

[67] Nitecki, p. 231.

[68] F.M. Salter, *Mediaeval Drama in Chester* (Toronto: University of Toronto Press, 1955), p. 104. Salter qualifies his statement by explaining that "in the Middle Ages God himself had a sense of humour and fully appreciated the absurd and ridiculous."

[69] Sinanoglou suggests that "to comprehend the impact of their brief visit to the Christ Child we must remember what wondrous effects were attributed by men of the fifteenth century to the sight of Christ in the host," p. 505.

[70] Munson, p. 62.

[71] Speyser, p. 17, concurs with Morgan, p. 681, that especially the *Prima Pastorum* places extraordinary emphasis on sight, culminating in this visual spectacle of the star.

CHAPTER 4:
Tense Comedy in the New Testament Plays

In the progression from the Nativity to later events of the New Testament, the cycle plays evince a marked difference in both the controlling tone and level of intensity. The prevailing emphasis is on serious attention to Christ's Ministry and Passion, subjects which comprise the most important thematic focus of the Corpus Christi cycles and include the dramatic scenes most likely to impress upon the spectators the necessity for repentance. In each of the cycles, the most vivid scenes are those which present in horrifying detail the slaughter of the innocents and the physical torment Christ suffered.

Any kind of comic intrusion on such tragic scenes seems terribly inappropriate, for comedy has the potential to diminish the emotional impact of human suffering. Yet one finds in these plays coarse jokes, inane secular games, and blatantly comic characterizations. Although one may theorize that such humor offers psychological release from the intensity of the drama,[1] this form of comedy provides no opportunity for relief and, in fact, does not evoke laughter or enjoyment. And unlike the buffoons one encounters in Elizabethan tragedy, the comic characters of these plays intensify--rather than soften--the appalling, violent enactment of suffering.

Because of the comic developments in these plays, the usual responses demanded by biblical accounts become more complex. In the Passion sequences, for example, although gruesome catalogues of Christ's suffering constituted an important late medieval tradition,[2] the cycle playwrights expand that tradition by demanding a more complicated emotional response. Comedy imposes a tension which prevents the spectators from moving too easily to a stance of _pathos_, of highly emotional--even blind--compassion for Christ. Shocking humor thus becomes a device which has the capacity for both sustaining emotional involvement and controlling the audience's response.

The result of this involvement is an acute, painful awareness of the differences between Christ and his tormentors, between the god-man and those who--like the spectators--remain only men. More importantly, these New Testament plays ridicule the corruption of the Old Law to the extent that the illogical New Law of Christ becomes the only rational means of overcoming chaos.

Massacre of the Innocents

Although the plays depicting the massacre of the innocents appear to be more appropriate in the context of the Nativity than in the Passion sequences, the controlling tone and theme of these plays immediately depart from the Nativity traditions and prepare the audience for the climax of the cycles. The source of humor in these plays is violent and disturbing, for the dramatic context--the random murder of infants--is not, of course, inherently comic. Unlike Mak's thievery or Noah's wrangling with his wife, the action here can scarcely be considered harmless fun. Yet several of the cycles use comic characterization and development to prepare the audience for the mixture of comic and grotesque elements that becomes intensified in the later New Testament plays.

Several comic features are common among the extant cycles and the Digby play of the massacre of the innocents. Except for the York Gyrdillers and Naylers' Play, all of the cycles characterize Herod's soldiers in comic terms. The knights--as they are called in the text--boast of their power and ruthlessness in battle. Although such swaggering is humorous in itself, the knights intensify the comedy by ironically reminding the audience that their dreaded foes are less than two years old. The Chester playwright is particularly adept in his ironic treatment of the knights' mission:

> If you will wytt what I height,
> my name is syr Waradrake the knight.
> Agaynst me dare no man fight,
> my dintes they so dreade.
>
> But fayne would I feight my fill,
> as fayne as facoune would flye,
> my lord to wreake at his will
> and make those dogges to dye.
> These congeons in there clowtes I will kill
> and stowtly with strokes them destroye.
> Shall never on skape by my will;
> all babbes for that boye, full sore shall they
> bye.
>
> (201-12)

Sir Waradrake and Sir Grymbald Lancherdeepe are able to overstate their bravery only because they know that their mission will be successful and that the usual risks of battle are not likely. An underlying cowardice emerges when one boasts under such safe circumstances, and the comic potential of this contrast is ably exploited by the dramatists.

The Towneley playwright, for example, exaggerates the

difference between the knights' perceived boldness and their actual cowardice by having them boast about the conflict which might have ensued had the three kings not eluded them:

<pre>
    primus Miles. Syr, thay went sodanly / or any
          man wyst,
    Els had mett we, yei, perdy / and may ye tryst.
    Secundus Miles. So bold nor so hardy / agans
          oure lyst,
    was none of that company / durst mete me with
          fyst
          ffor ferd.
    Tercius Miles. Ill durst thay abyde,
    Bot ran thame to hyde;
    Might I thaym haue spyde,
          I had made thaym a berd.
                                        (181-89)
</pre>

Because they are later hesitant to arm themselves for battle when Herod commands them, these knights reveal through their boasting a sense of relief that no actual confrontation ever occurred.

Furthermore, the Digby play focuses almost entirely on one character, Watkyn--Herod's young messenger--who is presented solely in comic terms. In his plea to be knighted, Watkyn pledges that he is "a man of myght"[3] who will ruthlessly fight Herod's battles, but his speeches belie such confident claims. His boasting about how he will slay the children, for example, is always undermined by his fear of the mothers and their distaffs:

<pre>
    And if I fynde a yong child I shall choppe it on
          a blokke;
    though the moder be angry, the child shalbe
          slayn,
    but yitt I drede no thyng more than a woman with
          a Rokke,
    ffor if I se ony suche, be my feith I come a-
          geyn.
                                        (157-60)
</pre>

175

Herod's reproof for such weakness forces Watkyn to avow that "And ther come an hundred women I wole not ffleen" (167), but his sudden display of boldness is comic in its insincerity. Although the subject itself is quite serious, the Digby playwright encourages the spectators to laugh at the bungling coward who wants the glory and power of knighthood without the danger that accompanies it.

Even the climactic moment of these plays--the confrontation between the knights and mothers and the inevitable slaying of the children--is anticipated with comic suspense, not dread of its horror. In Chester, the villainy of the murders is downplayed by Herod's command to "Dryve downe the dyrtie-arses all bydeene" (143) and by the knight's protest that men of their stature should not be required to "sley a shitten-arsed shrowe" (157). The comic aspect of the confrontation with the mothers is not suggested in the vaunts of Sir Waradrake and Sir Grymbald Lancherdeepe, but as soon as the knights meet the women and call them "queanes" (290), the stage is set for a humorous battle of wills. The spears of the knights are temporarily arrested by the insults and distaffs of the mothers:

PRIMUS MULIER
Whom callest thou 'queane,' scabde dogge?
Thy dame, thy daystard, was never syche.
Shee burned a kylne, eych stike;
yet did I never non.

SECUNDUS MULIER
Bee thou soe hardye, I thee behett,
to handle my sonne that is so sweete,
this distaffe and thy head shall meete
or wee heathen gonne.

(297-304)

176

Even the massacre itself is, on the surface, treated lightly in the Chester play, for the second knight explains Herod's order in terms of a game:

> Dame, thy sonne, in good faye,
> hee must of me learne a playe:
> hee must hopp, or I goe awaye,
> upon my speare ende.
>
> (321-24)

The serious connotation of this game is granted little space in the play.

Only the N-Town and York dramatists follow the expected pattern in portraying the mothers as piteous in their mourning and weeping; the other versions emphasize the rambunctious spirits of the mothers, even in the face of tragedy. In the Chester play, for example, the traditional lament of one mother --"My love, my lord, my life, my leife, / did never man or woman greiffe / to suffer such torment!" (330-32)--is immediately balanced by her physical retaliation as she beats the knight and commands him to "Beare the kinge this from me" (335).

Surprisingly, the comic focus remains unchanged even as the actual slaughter begins. Instead of an alarming, chaotic scene in which the knights quickly overpower the women and children, the dramatists deliberately choose a comic structure. Such emphasis is evident most clearly in the Chester play: Sir Wara-drake confronts and subdues the first mother, and then the action is repeated with Sir Grymbald Lancherdeepe's battle with the second mother. Even within these individual disputes, the dramatist is careful to keep the play from becoming melodramat-ic. The first mother's grief, for example, is checked by her barrage of insults and blows to the knight who has just slain her son:

> Have thou this, thou fowle harlott
> and thou knight, to make a knott!
> And on buffett with this bote
> thou shalt have to boote.
> And thow this, and thou this,
> though thou both shyte and pisse!
> And if thou thinke we doe amysse,
> goe buskes you to moote.
>
> (353-60)

And although she has already witnessed the death of a child, the second mother uses similar insults in an attempt to stave off the attacking knight. She even tries to deceive Sir Grymbald Lancherdeepe by claiming her son as a daughter and obscenely challenging him to prove her wrong (365-68).

A similar pattern is evident in the Towneley and Digby presentations of the Massacre of the Innocents. In Towneley, Herod himself warns his knights that they face their greatest danger "If women wax woode" (314), and the mothers do attack the knights in their one-on-one encounters. Watkyn's fear of the mothers becomes the focal point of the Digby play, for the actual slaughter is given far less attention than the women's attack on Watkyn. After Watkyn exposes his own wish to hide from the women, the play leads directly to this kind of confrontation:

I^a mulier.

> what, thu Iavell canst not haue do?
> thu and thi Cumpany shall not depart,
> tyll of our distavys ye haue take part:
> therfor, ley on gossippes with a mery hart,
> And lett them not from vs goo.
>   [here thei shall bete watkyn, and the
>   knyghtes shall come to rescue hym. . . .]
>   (345-49)

Although the dolls representing the dead infants presumably remain on stage, the whole scene explodes in lively farce. One may imagine that the mothers' revenge on Watkyn was allowed to play itself out for some time before the knights intervened and returned the scene to Herod.

In these plays, the dramatists reveal an acute sensitivity to the human response to violence and the strange relationship between horror and humor. Although even the idea of such a massacre is terrifying, people in the Middle Ages--presumably no less than those of the twentieth century--were drawn to witness the grotesque details of the crime. Much like our own explicit newspaper accounts of murder, rape, and torture, the descriptions of the massacre appeal simultaneously to the spectators' senses of fascination and repulsion. In N-Town, for example, Herod's order to kill the children is likely to have encouraged rapt attention, not overwhelming fear:

> It is tolde in grw
> his name xulde be jhesu
> i-fownde
> to haue hym ʒe gon
> hewe þe flesch with þe bon
> and gyf hym wownde
> Now kene knyghtys kythe ʒoure craftys
> and kyllyth knaue chylderyn and castyth hem in
> clay
> Shewyth on ʒour shulderys scheldys and schaftys
> Shapyht amonge schel chownys ashyrlyng shray
> doth rowncys rennyn with rakynge raftys
> tyl rybbys be to-rent with a reed ray
> lete no barne beleve on bete baftys
> tyl a beggere blede be bestys baye

(22-35)

The vivid action described in this passage is intensified by the speaker's brisk rhythm and harsh alliteration. And the speech moves rapidly from narration of the background to a resounding command that the knights prepare for relentlessness in battle.

Such a violent account is appropriate in characterizing Herod, but its placement in a farcical context inspires a complicated, mixed response from the spectators. The horror appears to be diminished but is, in fact, intensified; and the pleasurable scenes, which seem to be more enjoyable in the midst of grotesque action, are actually tinged with dread. The tension which results is both emotionally disquieting and dramatically appealing.[4]

The characterization of Herod elicits similar responses, for in him the comic features often seen in a proud man are merged with the terrifying traits of an amoral madman in a position of power. In all of the cycles, Herod rants before the spectators as he asserts his might and threatens those who challenge his authority. In menacing tones and specific, violent threats against those who defy him, Herod reveals his vaunting pride and his unwavering belief in his own invincibility. His opening speech in the Digby play, for example, is comic in its presentation of self-glorification:

> what erthely wretches with pompe & pride
> do a-geyns my lawes or with-stonde myn entent,
> thei shall suffre woo and peyne thurgh bak and
>   syde,
> With a very myschaunce ther flesshe shalbe all
>   to-rent.
> And all my ffoes shall haue suche commaundement
> that they shalbe glad to do my byddyng; Ay,
> Or elles thei shalbe in woo and myscheff
>   permament,
> that thei shall fere me nyght and day.
>   (73-80)

Herod's empty threats and his exaggerations of power are amusing, even though what he proposes is violent and irrational. Even the Towneley play, in which Herod accuses the spectators directly and tries to intimidate them, has a comic appeal. He warns them to listen to him or else he will "breake ilka bone, / And pull fro the skyn / the carcas anone" (84-85), and the typical request for the audience to be quiet is similarly overstated:

> Peasse both yong and old / at my bydyng, I red,
> ffor I haue all in wold / in me standys lyfe and
> dede;
> who that is so bold / I brane hym thrugh the
> hede;
> Speke not or I haue told / what I will in this
> stede;
> ye wote nott
> All that I will mefe;
> Styr not bot ye haue lefe,
> ffor if ye do, I clefe
> you small as flesh to pott.
>
> (91-99)

If there were real danger in these threats, the spectators would not be amused; however, the safety of the actor-audience relationship allows a more objective response to the laughable incongruities of Herod's claims. His lack of reason is ludicrous, for he resorts to extreme physical abuse as the logical punishment for a person who has interrupted him. And the extremes to which Herod must go to maintain his power serve only to undermine his authority.

By no means, however, is Herod a comic figure. Although he is humorously presented as an indomitable ruler--one whose fall from power is imminent--his speeches also reveal his terrifying ruthlessness in his desire to preserve his reign at any cost.

In Towneley, his anger toward the infant Christ is inhuman in its objective cruelty: "It mefys my hart right noght / To breke his nek in two" (125-26). In Chester, Herod's logical explanation of the reason for the massacre is chilling--but comically chilling--in that it calmly transfers blame from Herod to Christ:

> But syth it may noe other bee
> but these kinges are gone from me,
> and that shrewe would have my soveraintye,
> I thinke to put him agayne:
> all the knave-children in this contree
> shall by his guile, soe mote I thee.
> Because I knowe not which is hee,
> all for his sake shalbe slayne.
>
> (33-40)

His reasoning is laughable, but the situation is not: unlike the idle threats which are intended to quiet the crowd, this directive leads to senseless, random slaughter.

The characterizations of Herod--like the portrayals of the knights and their battles with the mothers--maintain this underlying tension. As a result, the plays teeter uneasily on the brink between horror and fascination, _pathos_ and comedy. Such a position presents several dramatic and thematic advantages over the more stylized York treatment.

First, the playwrights encourage a more energetic emotional response than the tender compassion one might feel toward murdered children. The sense of outrage and disgust which is inherent in the plays' violence is tempered by reminders that Herod and his soldiers are simply weak mortals with limited judgment. On a dramatic level, such controlled involvement intensifies the sense of growing danger which begins after the joyful Nativity scenes. The plays thus constitute an important step in the emotional preparation for the Passion.

Secondly, the precarious balance of comic and horrifying events in these plays places the spectators in a suitable position to understand the central theme of the Passion sequences which follow: the differences between the Old and New Laws. Herod's reign is an example of the corruption of the Old Law, for his authority is upheld only through intimidation, and he deludes himself about the earthly limits of his own power. Although God's vengeance is literally introduced only in the N-Town personification of death, the spectators are not allowed to forget that the wickedness of this temporal kingdom will not go unpunished. And although the soldiers are armed with spears and orders to kill, the unstated power of the New Law causes them to fail, and, for the time being, Christ escapes the folly of human perception.

One may argue that such comic irony is at the heart of the New Law, for Christ's teachings and life are filled with apparent incongruities: in poverty, one is wealthy; in weakness, one is strong; and in dying, one lives forever.[5] More important in the mystery cycles, however, is the relationship between mundane, low comedy and the high spiritual plane of the New Law. The games played with the children in Chester, for example, amplify the horror of their crime, for the soldiers are too involved in their own amusement to see the overall picture. Their blindness in following the commands of a maniacal earthly ruler is startling in its lack of moral conviction, and their ineptitude is humorous only to a point. As a result, the theme of the New Law and its subtle strength is reinforced by a chaotic tone which continues through the New Testament plays.

The Passion Plays

The presentation of the Passion sequences in the mystery cycles grows out of a rich medieval tradition of contemplating Christ's suffering. In the late Middle Ages, both art and literature reflected this tradition, often through graphic—even grotesque—representations of the Crucifixion. The tendency in art was ". . . a turning to immediate experience, to detail, to individuality as sources for affective art."[6] The appeal of such portrayals is at times intellectual, for medieval artists, in particular, made extensive use of the symbolism of Christ and the Crucifixion. More often, however, the writers and artists appealed to the hearts of their audiences and sought to elicit highly emotional responses. This early fourteenth-century lyric, for example, emphasizes the personal torment the speaker feels in contemplating the Crucifixion:

> When I thee beholde,
> With eyen brighte bo,
> And thy body colde,
> Thy ble waxeth blo;
> Thou hengest all of blode,
> So heye upon the Rode,
> Betwene theves two.
> Who may sike more? [7]

A similar surge of feeling is expressed in the following burden of a fourteenth-century carol, in which the speaker focuses on a tear in Christ's eye:

> Lovely ter of lovely eiye,
> Why dostu me so wo?

Sorful ter of sorful eiye,[8]
Thu brekst mine herte ato.

Emotional portrayals of Mary's suffering at the sight of her crucified son show similar appeals to the hearts of the readers. The pieta tradition in art--in which Mary cradles her dead son in her lap--informs this fifteenth-century complaint, for example, by emphasizing sentimental maternal emotions:

O! woman, thou takest thy childe by the hand,
And seyste, 'Dere sone, gif me a stroke.'
My sonis handes ar so bledand
To loke on them me liste not to layke.
His handes he sufferd for thy sake
Thus to be bored with nailes sere.
When thou makes mirth gret sorows I make,
For now lyeth dedd my dere sone, dere.[9]

As Davies explains, this poem "fully and poignantly explores the heartbreaking potentialities of a situation chosen for its sentimental power."[10]

The cycle playwrights, also emphasizing emotional responses to the events of the Passion, had several advantages over other writers and artists. The intense dramatic situation offered by skillful staging charged the plays with a dynamism that is impossible in pictorial representations or sermons. A carefully timed pace, for example, would allow the Passion sequences to begin at twilight and proceed toward the Crucifixion as the last rays of daylight extinguished. Medieval paintings often depicted the gruesome details of Christ's death, such as the strain of the torturers in stretching his limbs to fit the holes already bored in the cross; the cycle playwrights could achieve even more spectacular realism by adding to the visual image the horrible sound of the hammering and the overwhelming sense of chaos.[11] The central _platea_ that is clearly evident in the N-Town cycle allows for a complex stage with two or more actions occurring simultaneously.[12] And the extensive interaction with the spectators--who are, at times, cast in the role of the throngs in Jerusalem--demands that the audience participate in, not merely observe, the events on stage. Through the skillful adaptation of source material, the dramatists were able to transform the narration of Christ's trial and death into a series of tense, fast-paced, involving plays which consistently emphasize both the desperate need for the New Law and the subtle strength of that Law.

One of the crucial sources of dramatic strength in the cycles is the detailed, often humorous characterization of the traditional villains, especially Herod, Pilate, and Judas. In several of the plays, Herod and Pilate are developed comically, for they struggle between the possibility of looking foolish and the importance of judging Christ's case properly. The Chester play of the trial of Christ, for example, clearly presents such a dilemma in spite of the fact that Pilate and Herod have relatively few lines. They are eager to maintain peace among the people by the usual methods of counsel, but they become frustrated when these methods only complicate the situation. Direct questioning results in equivocal answers or silence from Christ, and Pilate's plan to pass responsibility to Herod also fails.

Although the failure itself is not comic, Pilate's relentlessness in trying the case with reason and justice appears silly since Annas and Caiaphas are determined to have their way.

He responds to cries of "nayle him, nayle him to the crosse" (220) with an impotent scolding: "Yee men, for shame! Lett bee your noyce!" (221). His reminder of the tradition of delivering a prisoner is equally ineffective, but Pilate desperately continues his appeals to the crowds. After washing his hands as a symbolic reminder that he is innocent of wanting to shed "this rightwise mans bloodd" (242), Pilate pleads with Christ to clear himself and tries to use reason to understand the enigmatic answers he receives. As the following passage reveals, the two men speak on completely different levels:

> JESUS
> And if my realme in this world were,
> stryve I would with you nowe here
> and lead with me such powere
> should pryve you of your praye.
> But my might in this manere
> will I not prove, ne nowe appere
> as worldly kinge; my cause uncleare
> were then, in good faye.
>
> PILATUS
> Ergo, a kinge thou art, or was.
>
> JESUS
> That thou sayes, yt is no lesse.
> But nowe I tell thee here expresse
> that kinge I am and be maye.
> In world I came to beare wytnes
> of soothnes, and therfore borne I was,
> and all that leeven soothnes
> take heede to that I saye.
>
> (267-82)

The incongruity of their planes of thought is ironic, and the spectators would recognize in such a discussion both the germ of the Christian mystery and the impossibility of proving that mystery through reason.

More blatantly comic is the attitude adopted by both Pilate

and Herod when their usual methods fail. When Christ stands silently before Herod, the ruler's curiosity quickly turns to sarcasm as he overstates his perception that Christ must be mad:

Methinkes this man is wonders throo,
dombe and deafe as a doted doo,
or frenticke, in good faye.

. . .

Cloth him in white, for in this case
to Pilate hit may be solace,
for Jewes custome before was
to cloth men that were wood
or madd, as nowe hee him mase,
as well seemes by his face;
for him that hase lost his grace
this garment is full good.

(187-202)

And when Annas reminds Pilate that "whoso calles himselfe a kinge here / reves Caesar of his power" (303-04), Pilate's patience and diligence are cast aside. Because he has just proclaimed that he can find no cause for damnation, Pilate's vicious command seems humorous in its abruptness and vehemence: "Anone goe scourge this losingere / and beat him lymme and lythe" (305-07).

Of course, such a joke—the implausibly rapid overthrow of compassion—cannot be classified with the raucous humor one finds elsewhere in the cycles, since the humor itself is less developed and the dramatic context is morbidly serious. Unlike the comic effect achieved in the earlier episodes, the uneasy yoking of comic and profound elements here produces more than emotional involvement and yearning for resolution; it creates and sustains a sense of chaos, both on stage and in the minds of the spectators.[13] In this confusion, everything is turned on its head. Raving reveals weakness instead of strength. The old laws of authority seem to be in effect, but are actually ineffective. And clever insults and jests are simply not funny. Such inversion is possible because the figure of Christ calmly, silently stands in contrast to the tumult about him. Ironically, he is at once both victim and victor, slave and savior, of the misguided men who abuse him.

This contrast is more clearly evident in the York treatment of Pilate and Herod and in the Towneley dramatization of the conspiracy against Christ. In these plays, biblical and secular source materials are expanded to widen the gulf between Christ and the rulers who judge him. Based on passages in Matthew and Luke, the York cycle, like the N-Town, includes the dream of Pilate's wife as an important dramatic development. The York playwright, however, uses this scene not only to reveal Satan's attempt to prevent the Crucifixion, but also to glance satirically at those who judge Christ.

The intimate opening scene between Pilate and his wife, Percula, marks an abrupt quelling of the riotous play which preceded it; for instead of the monumental occasion of Christ's buffeting, the Tapiteres and Couchers' play focuses on a tranquil domestic scene. As they greet one another politely, Pilate compliments his "worthely wiffe" (26) on her beauty, and Percula praises her "duke doughty" (29) for his power and skill in judgment. Such courtly manners are cast aside, however, in the York playwright's elaboration on the sensuality of Percula and its effect on Pilate. She describes her own beauty and stature as "þe prise" (37) of Pilate with as much seductive as proud intentions, as if to remind her husband of his good fortune:

> All welle of all womanhede I am, wittie and wise,
> Consayue nowe my countenaunce so comly & clere.
> the coloure of my corse is full clere,
> And in richesse of robis am I rayed,
> Ther is no lorde in þis londe as I lere,
> In faith þat hath a frendlyar feere,
> Than yhe my lorde,
> My-selffe yof I saye itt.
>
> (39-45)

As one might expect, Pilate takes the bait. Despite the formal setting of Pilate's court, the self-indulgence of the couple is given further development.[14] Their compliments to one another are entirely sexual:

> Pil. Howe! howe! felawys, nowe in faith I am
>   fayne
> Of theis lippis, so loffely are lappid,
> In bedde is full buxhome and bayne.
>
> Domina. Yha, sir, it nedith not to layne,
> All ladise we coveyte þan
> Bothe to be kyssed and clappid.
>
> (50-54)

The timely intrusion of the beadle at this point interferes with the seduction but not with the comic development of the scene. Percula angrily dismisses the "horosonne boy" (60), even though he appropriately reminds them of proper conduct in court; and in spite of his recognition that the beadle is right, Pilate invites his wife to drink wine with him before she leaves. The festive tone continues in the high court when their intemperance necessitates that Percula be escorted home by her son and Pilate helped to bed by the beadle.

No outside interference seems able to penetrate the security and pleasure of Pilate and his circle. Yet all the while this harmless revelry in presented on stage, the spectators know that this is the court in which Christ is to be judged, and that the innocuous playing will give way to violence and turmoil. As a result, the enjoyment of the domestic scene is riddled with tension, and the audience awaits the bustling interruption of the crowds who will bring Christ to court.

Surprisingly, it is Satan--not Caiaphas--who intrudes first. Whereas Satan's visitation to Pilate's wife in the N-Town play is enacted silently and revealed only in a stage direction, the York version makes his warning audible, and he appeals to Percula's sense of pride in their worldly power and wealth, not to her fear of eternal damnation:

> Sir Pilate, for his prechyng, and þou,
> With nede schalle ye namely be noyed,
> Your striffe and youre strenghe schal be stroyed,
> Youre richesse schal be refte you þat is rude,
> With vengeaunce, and þat dare I auowe.
>
> (172-76)

To Percula, the threat of such losses is serious and disconcerting, but not because of spiritual considerations. The York dramatist once again succeeds in disquieting the spectators through comic irony, for Percula's limited focus on earthly possessions completely obstructs her moral and religious conscience; she is not, however, a viciously evil character, and her befuddled alarm at the dream is comic in the dramatic context of her drunkenness upon retiring.

Another important comic intrusion upon these serious scenes is the treatment of Herod. Whereas the N-Town and Chester dramatists present him as a stock character whose action is dominated by pride, the York playwright widens his focus on the king, allowing him to play games with Christ and to inflict humiliation as well as physical abuse. Like the opening scene in Pilate's court, the first glimpse of Herod reveals the king's perception of his own power and his insistence on the luxury and physical comfort afforded by his high estate. Even as he begins his opening speech, however, Herod discloses a more violent temper, a more vindictive spirit, than Pilate. He threatens the audience with explicit descriptions of the punishment that awaits traitors:

> Traueylis noȝt as traytours þat tristis in
>   trayne,
> Or by þe bloode þat mahounde bledde, with þis
>   blad schal ye blede.
> Pus schall I brittyn all youre bones on brede,
>   ae,
> And lusshe all youre lymmys with lasschis.
> Dragons þat are dredfull schall derke in þer
>   denne
> In wrathe when we writhe, or in wrathenesse are
>   wapped,
> Agaynst jeauntis on-gentill haue we joined with
>   ingendis,
> And swannys þat are swymmyng to oure swetnes
>   schall be suapped,
> And joged doune þer jolynes oure gentries
>   engenderand;
> Who so repreue oure estate we schall choppe þam
>   in cheynes.
>
>   (7-16)

The alliteration which is characteristic of the York Realist here serves to accentuate the resounding force of Herod's vile threats. His sadistic enjoyment in elaborating the details of the tortures is horrifying, particularly because Pilate has just placed responsibility for Christ's life in the hands of this sinister despot.

192

Such an opening is intended to confirm the spectators' fear of and contempt for Herod, and the subsequent emphasis on the king's own pleasure—such as Herod's reminder that he is "full tendirly hydid" (51)—is treated sarcastically. The dramatist complicates such an impression, however, by revealing Herod's more humorous side. The appearance of Christ in Herod's hall is considered "a presente fro Pilate" (98), a gift which the messenger tells Herod "will heffe vppe youre hertis" (97). This view of the trial as a game enacted for the enjoyment of the king is sustained even in the actual encounter with Christ, and the result is a carnival-like atmosphere in which all seems to be trivial amusement but is actually highly serious.

As soon as he sees Christ, Herod extends a playful welcome, addressing Christ in French: "Saie! beene venew in bone fay, / Ne plesew et a parle remoy" (146-47). The essential tension is immediately highlighted, however, in the messenger's suggestion that such a tone is inappropriate, since "he can of no bourdyng, þis boy" (148). Unlike the intellectual curiosity Herod initially has toward Christ in the Chester and N-Town cycles, the York character welcomes Christ's visit as an opportunity for sport:

> O! my harte hoppis for joie
> To se nowe þis prophette appere,
> We schall haue goode game with þis boy,
> Takis hede, for in haste ȝe schall here.
> I leve we schall laugh and haue likyng
> To se nowe þis lidderon her he leggis oure lawis.
> (164-67)

The subsequent treatment of Christ reflects Herod's playful attitude, as the messengers marvel at Christ's inappropriate behavior before a king, and Herod feigns wonder as he hears about the miracles of the loaves and fishes and the raising of Lazarus.[15]

Were it not Christ who was the brunt of Herod's jokes, the spectators might be moved to laughter as the king rants in strange tongues, presumably with great animation and exaggerated giddiness:

> Howe likis þa? wele, lorde? saie, what! deuyll
> neuere a dele?
> I faute in my reuerant in otill moy,
> I am of fauour, loo! fairer be ferre.
> Kyte oute yugilment, vta! oy! oy!
> Be any witte þat y watte it will waxe werre.
> Seruicia primet such losellis and lurdaynes as
> þou, loo!
> Respicias timet, what þe deuyll and his dame
> schall y now doo?
>
> (231-37)

The silence with which Christ responds serves only to vex Herod further, and he plunges into his playful mockery with even greater force. Instead of merely speaking to Christ as if he were royalty, Herod gives him a sceptre and parades the implausible figure before his court. Such provocation becomes boring to Herod, however, when Christ remains passive, neither rebelling against nor participating in the game.

Although Christ does not speak throughout this play, his presence speaks the ineffable power with which the unwitting Herod toys. The king's playful verbal attacks, the sight gag of robing an assumed fool as a king, and the "foule noyse" (320) of the commotion in the court coalesce to form a well-developed joke. Within the play, Christ is the object of that humor, and Herod and his company mistakenly believe that they have had the last laugh. In the larger dramatic context, however, the spectators are aware that the presentation of Christ as a king is not a joke at all. Through the comic surface and tone of the play, the York dramatist succeeds in illustrating vividly and feelingly the contrast between brash earthly perceptions of authority and the impervious strength implied in the Christian concept of power.

This contrast is even more strikingly presented in the Towneley <u>Conspiracio,</u> where the desperate, fiendish plotting of corrupt earthly rulers is directly juxtaposed to the humble stance of Christ at the Last Supper. The tightly organized play focuses sharply on this contrast as it moves briskly from the conspiracy to the capture of Christ. In keeping with the cohesiveness of the play, the Towneley dramatist eliminates the characterization of Herod and magnifies the power and wiliness of Pilate.

In addition to traditional assertions of might, Pilate casually alludes to his own abuse of power. The references to men of court is satiric, since his description of their falseness applies equally to medieval, as well as historical, courts:

> ffor I am he that may / make or mar a man;
> My self if I it say / as men of cowrte now can;
> Supporte a man to day / to-morn agans hym than,
> On both parties thus I play / And fenys me to
> > ordan
> > The right;
> Bot all fals indytars,
> Quest mangers and Iurers,
> And all thise fals out rydars,
> > Ar welcom to my sight.

> (19-27)

Through such a startling revelation of his lack of moral conviction in court, Pilate immediately dismisses what might be an important motive in eliminating Christ. He obviously detests Christ not on the grounds that he considers him to be a false prophet, but because he fears that "if he lyf a yere / dystroy oure law must vs" (38). Thus the necessity of upholding the current law motivates Pilate--as well as Caiaphas and Annas--to seek to destroy Christ.

The tone of the entire play is derisive, in that the rulers' insistence on the sanctity of the Old Law is undermined by their own corruption. Caiaphas reminds the council that "oure law now must vs lere" (57), not to find a means to administering justice but to discover "som preuay poynt" (72) on which to incriminate Christ. Their choices of evidence against Christ are often expressed ironically, since--as in the following passage--Christ's good works are stated to be in defiance of their law:

> <u>Cayphas</u>. Sir, I can rekyn you on a raw
>   a thowsand wonders, and well moo,
> Of crokyd men, that we well knaw,
>   how graythly that he gars them go,
> And euer he legys agans oure law,
>   tempys oure folk and turnys vs fro.
>
>   (92-97)

Such comic self-exposure abounds in this play, as Pilate and the priests reveal the emptiness which motivates their loyalty to the law.

The Towneley dramatist also treats Judas' offer to sell Christ with comic irony. In justifying his demand for thirty pence as a selling price for Christ, Judas intends to demonstrate not only the wrongs Christ has done but also his own skill in reason. Pilate, Annas, and Caiaphas praise him and agree to his terms, but the audience would not miss seeing the hypocrisy and selfish motivation behind his betrayal. As this passage illustrates, Judas' haughty criticism of Christ's disregard for the poor is immediately contrasted with his revelation that he had intended to make a profit from the sale of Mary Magdalen's precious ointment:

> I sayd it was worthy to sell
>   thre hundreth pens in oure present,
> ffor to parte poore men emell;
>   bot will ye se wherby I ment?
> The tent parte, truly to tell,
>   to take to me was myne intent;
> ffor of the tresure that to vs fell,
>   the tent parte euer with me went;
> And if thre hundreth be right told,
>   the tent parte is euen thryrty;
> Right so he shalbe sold;
>   say if ye will hym by.
>
> (270-81)

The crime itself is heinous, but the unwitting self-exposure of the criminal is bitterly comic. Certainly, one would not expect a hilarious response from the spectators at the conclusion of this scene, but clearly the playwright is working to elicit a broader range of responses than simple hatred of the evil characters.

Also included in the Conspiracio is the traditional presentation of the Last Supper, a scene which is the inversion of the previous action in tone and pace, as well as in content. Although a much larger group is assembled on stage for this scene, the action is much calmer, much more focused than the frenetic scheming of Pilate, Annas, and Caiaphas. The mood that is established reinforces the theological emphasis on this scene.

The New Law, the Christian law of love, is not only explained; it is dramatically enacted.

As they gather for the meal, Christ announces to his disciples the principle on which his law is based: "If I be master I will be brothere" (351). This position is affirmed in the image of Christ's kneeling before the disciples to wash their feet, as he explains, "Sen I, both lord and master, to you wold knele / to wesh youre fete, so must ye wele" (406-07). His brief outline of profound religious mysteries--Resurrection, heaven, the Trinity--befuddles the disciples. The spectators, however, would recognize immediately the acute contrast between this genuinely powerful law and the corrupt, self-serving law of those who conspire against Christ. Certainly, the dramatic situation is highly serious, but the direct juxtaposition of Pilate's hall to the scene of the Last Supper accentuates the incongruity of the two laws as it slowly, deliberately mocks those who cannot see the petty limits of their earthly power.

The uneasiness produced by such expanded comic developments on the brink of the central tragic focus of the cycles reveals the playwrights' perception of a useful emotional stance for the audience. The spectators know the biblical story and already have strong alliances with its suffering "hero" and equally strong rejection of those who judge and torment him. By rounding out the characters of the traditional villains and by controlling the tone of the plays, the dramatists complicate the traditional audience response to Christ's Passion and Crucifixion. Because of this intellectual complexity, the spectators are encouraged to respond to the play on a completely emotional level. And in such a state, the often grotesque details of the Crucifixion are likely to inspire profound compassion for Christ, as well as guilt for their human responsibility in his suffering.

Even more horrifying than their explicit counterparts in medieval art, the Passion sequences of the cycle plays relentlessly bombard the spectators with vivid and violent details of Christ's suffering and death. Paradoxically, much of the lively dramatic action seems to focus attention away from the central event, the Crucifixion. The stage character of Christ is a literal translation of biblical accounts, and there are few surprises in his traditional pronouncements from the cross. The crowds around him, however, are boldly rounded out, as they swarm around their passive prey. And although one may expect such strong character development as a means of evoking contempt, the comic action of these scenes is shocking in its proximity to the profound divine mystery of the Crucifixion.

The second play of the N-Town Passion sequence, for example, offers precise stage directions to the actors who are cast as Jews. No specific dialogue is indicated for much of the action, but one may well imagine the coarse comments which accompany this scene:

> here pylat xal rysyn and gon to his schaffalde,
> and þe busshoppys with hym and þe jewys xul crye
> for joy with a gret voys and Arryn hym and
> pullyn of his clothis and byndyn hym to A pelere
> and skorgyn hym on seyng þus
>
> i^{us} judeus
>
> Doth gladly oure kyng
> for þis is our fyrst begynnyng.   (676-77)

> and qwan he is skorgyd þei put upon hym A cloth
> of sylk and settyn hym on a stol and puttyn A
> kroune of þornys on hese hed with forkys and þe
> jewys knelyng to cryst takyng hym A septer and
> skornyng hym and þan þei xal pullyn of þe purpyl
> cloth and don on A-geyn his owyn clothis and leyn
> þe crosse in hese necke to berynt and drawyn hym
> forth with ropys

The most shocking aspect of their attitude is the spirit with which they carry out the torture prescribed by Pilate. The reasons for the punishment seem to have been forgotten, for instead of presenting righteous men with conviction of Christ's wrongdoing, the playwright portrays the Jews as unswerving sadists, who remember only enough of Christ's teaching to use in mocking him. When they reach Calvary, the torturers pragmatically rehearse the formula for a proper crucifixion and interject prosaic comments on Christ's misfortune and their own physical prowess and ingenuity:

ij[us] judeus

> pul hym down evyl mote he the
> And gyf me his arm in hast
> And A-non we xal se
> hese good days þei xul be past.

iij[us] judeus

> Gef hese other Arm to me
> A-nother take hed to hese feet
> And A-non we xal se
> yf þe borys be for hym meet.

iiij[us] judeus

> þis is mete take good hede
> pulle out þat Arm to þe sore.

i[us] judeus

> þis is short þe deuyl hym sped
> be a large fote and more.

ij[us] judeus

> Ffest on A Rop and pulle hym long
> and I xal drawe þe A-geyn
> spare we not þese ropys strong

200

> þow we brest both flesch and veyn.
>
> iij[us] judeus
>
> dryve in þe nayl a-non   lete se
> And loke and þe flesch and senues well last.
>
> iiij[us] judeus
>
> þat I graunt so mote I the
> lo þis nayl is dreve ryth wel and fast.
>
> (730-49)

The enactment of such a grisly scene is disturbing in itself, but the objective cruelty of the Jews further increases the capacity of the scene to stir strong emotion. And their comic attention to detail is painful since they rigidly follow the rules without questioning whether the game itself is appropriate. As Kolve suggests, "the tortores are dramatized as too self-aware, too conscious of their own need for amusement, distraction, and gratification, to be more than sporadically aware of the man they kill."[16]

The Chester dramatist expands the game by including the competition for Christ's clothes. After comforting the weeping women he passes, Christ must wait with his cross while the Jews argue about the rules of the dice game and the proper division of his coat. More than eighty lines of the Passion play comically develop their arguments, and tension builds as this diversion becomes the central action of the scene. Even the disruption of their game is blatantly comic, since Caiaphas, in disbelief, reminds the Jews of the other, more important game:

> Men, for cockes face,
> howe longe shall pewee-ars
> stand naked in that place?
> Goe nayle him on the tree!
>
> (149-52)

Were it not Christ who is the victim of this joke, were he not the nude person who calmly waits to be noticed, Caiaphas' interruption would be hilarious. The dramatic context, however, deflates even this richly timed quip, and the sheer humor of his obscene reference intensifies the spectators' repulsion.[17]

The childish antics of the torturers continue throughout the Crucifixion. The swaggering which is suggested in the N-Town cycle is much more explicit in Chester, since the Jews clamor for Pilate's admiration and blessing. And the boasts about their physical ability almost lead to another argument before Pilate intercedes.

The Towneley Passion plays, however, surpass the other cycles in their horrifying depiction of physical and psychological torment and their detailed treatment of the Jews. Consistent with the dominant theme of understanding the New Law, the Towneley dramatist characterizes the torturers as rigid conformists to a game which has little meaning for them. Like children who insist on playing by the rules--even if those rules are irrational or not understood--the Jews abide by the dictates of a corrupt law. They randomly invent one game after another as they lead Christ toward Calvary, but their jests, unlike those of Herod, are not motivated by a need for amusement. Instead, the torturers blindly, merrily follow the prescribed steps in a traditional game. They have neither the sense nor the inclination to consider where such sport leads.

In the _Coliphizacio_, the dramatist is particularly adept at turning the law itself into a game. Caiaphas abuses his posi-

202

tion of power and remarks that such violations are commonplace: "whoso kepis the lawe, I gess, / he gettis more by purches / Then bi his fre rent" (160-62). He names Christ "kyng copyn in oure game" (166) and seems to enjoy producing a torrent of curses and accusations. In his overreaction to the silence with which Christ responds, Caiaphas viciously fantasizes about the punishment that Christ deserves.

Annas' gentle reminders of the law provide a comic foil for these violent pronouncements, and one may imagine Caiaphas here as an overpowering bully who is barely restrained by these weak appeals to his conscience:

> Cayphas. Now fowll myght hym befall!
> Anna. Sir, ye ar vexed at all,
> And perauentur he shall
>   here after pleas you;
>
> we may bi oure law / examyn hym fyrst.
> Cayphas. Bot I gif hym a blaw / my hart will
>   brist.
> Anna. Abyde to ye his purpose knaw. /
> Cayphas.   nay, bot I shall out
>   thrist
> Both his een on a raw.
>
>   . . .
>
> Cayphas. Shall I neuer ete bred / to that he be
>   stald
>   In the stokys.
> Anna. Sir, speke soft and styll,
> let vs do as the law will.
> Cayphas. Nay, I myself shall hym kyll,
>   And murder with knokys.
>
>   (186-94; 202-07)

The banter of the high priests is reminiscent of the dialogue between Cain and Abel. Annas' reminder, "It is best that we trete hym / with farenes" (217), is lost amid the shouts and threats of Caiaphas, and the playful shifting of tones is well balanced and enjoyable. The subject matter, however, does not allow the same response as in the Old Testament plays, for here the dispute is based not on the necessity of tithing, but on the proper use of the law in judging Christ. Annas passively awaits evidence of Christ's guilt, whereas Caiaphas, assuming that Christ is guilty, relies on the law only as a means of determining brutal enough punishment. Their dispute thus evokes more discomfort than pleasure because the spectators know that Annas will yield and, more importantly, because the victim of these abuses is Christ.

The actual buffeting scene elaborately develops a similar tension. The exuberance of Caiaphas is exaggerated in comic detail, as he rants about the punishment he wants to inflict. He even regrets his stature as a clerk, "Els myght I haue made vp wark / of yond harlot and mare" (310). His comic manipulation of the law is emphasized in his last plea to Annas, for his motivation is ambiguously expressed:

> Bot certys, or he hens yode,
> It wold do me som good
> To se knyghtys knok his hoode
>   with knokys two or thre.
>
> ffor sen he has trespast / and broken oure law,
> let vs make hym agast / and set hym in awe.
> (312-17)

The personal satisfaction Caiaphas seeks in buffeting Christ far outweighs his sense of obligation in upholding the law, for Christ's crime is mentioned only as weak rationalization for a game Caiaphas has no intention of abandoning. Once Annas consents, Caiaphas reiterates their personal motivation with his whooping cheer to the knights: "yei, syrs, and for my sake / Gyf hym good payment" (323-24).

The knights further blur the distinction between revenge and justice in the "new play of yoyll" (344) which they play with Christ. In addition to boasts by the knights about how they will "clowt well his kap" (335), the playwright maintains a comic tone through the introduction of the servant, Froward. Like other servants in the cycles--such as Garcio in the Cain and Abel plays--Froward is bold and argumentative. When commanded to fetch a stool, he leads the knights into a dispute over the more effective position for buffeting, and he rebels similarly when sent for a veil. The playfulness of the servant is further accentuated in his complaint to the first torturer that "I haue had mekyll shame / hunger and thurst, / In youre seruyce" (382-83). Unlike the cheekiness of Cain's servant, however, Froward's saucy complaint is a reminder of an even greater audacity, since his own shame is nothing compared to the suffering they have already begun to inflict on Christ.

In this dramatic context, Christ's silence reverberates through their games more loudly than the torturers' taunts. Their witless jests--such as the blind man's buff game--are no longer funny, for the attention of the audience is relentlessly directed toward the blindfolded, seated victim.[18] And their mockery unsettles rather than amuses, as this passage illustrates:

> primus tortor. Thus shall we hym refe / all his
>   fonde talys.
> Secundus tortor. Ther is noght in thi nefe / or
>   els this hart falys.

> ffroward. I can my hand vphefe / and knop out the
> skalys.
> primus tortor. Godys forbot ye lefe / bot set in
> youre nalys
> On raw.
> Sit vp and prophecy.
> ffroward. Bot make vs no ly.
> Secundus tortor. who smote the last?
> primus tortor.   was it I?
> ffroward. he wote not, I traw.
>
> (406-14)

Part of the discomfort evoked by this scene stems from the controlled irony that is so apparent in this game. The knights presume that they have mastery over Christ, a seemingly blind and helpless victim. The spectators know, however, that the spiritual blindness of the torturers is much more disabling than the veil tied over Christ's eyes. The audience also knows that Christ himself is playing a role in a much more serious and significant game than the torturers realize. The raucous closing of the play, in which the knights boast to Caiaphas that they "had almost / knokyd hym on slepe" (422-23), further emphasizes this spiritual blindness. In spite of their confrontation with Christ and their ironically appropriate treatment of him as a king, the group is completely unchanged. With insults and jeering, the knights herd Christ off to Pilate; Froward once more complains about his role as a servant; and Caiaphas frets "lest pylate for mede / let ihesus go" (435). The sources of comedy in the play thus become the sources of horror, for the torturers' playfulness in the face of profound suffering is more terrifying, more repulsive, than the torture itself. And emotional involvement intensifies as the cycle moves quickly, inevitably, toward the Crucifixion.

The staging of the Crucifixion has tremendous dramatic potential in all of the cycles, but the careful weaving of comic threads throughout the Towneley Passion sequences creates an even greater possibility for complex involvement on the part of the audience. The sarcastic crowning and worship of Christ in the Fflagellacio play is expanded in horrible detail in the Processus cruci to create a hauntingly festive atmosphere. Even the opening speeches of Pilate and the torturers are more menacing, more wild than the usual pleas for silence from the spectators. Their accusations against Christ, "this fals chuffer here" (31), are pronounced with such myopic conviction as to make the torturers appear drunk, for their tone has both the vehemence and the frivolity so common to that state. And like drunkards, the torturers perform every task in exaggerated detail.

One of the most elaborate jests is their insistence that Christ "Iust in tornamente" (92) as proof of his high station. With relentless taunting and ridicule, the torturers present Christ with his cross as if they were helping their king to mount a horse:

> iiijus tortor. Stand nere, felows, and let se
> how we can hors oure kyng so fre,
>   By any craft;
> Stand thou yonder on yond syde,
> And we shall se how he can ryde,
>   And how to weld a shaft.
>
> primus tortor. Sir, commys heder and haue done,
> And wyn apon youre palfray sone,
>   ffor he [is] redy bowne.
>
> (107-15)

In their enactment of what they consider a clever and cruel

metaphor, the torturers unwittingly remind the audience of the popular medieval icon of Christ as a rescuing knight, an image which "normally serves as a demonstration of the humiliation and suffering that Christ endured for love of man."[19] To the torturers, the joke is hilarious precisely because the image of a knight is so incongruous with the battered man before them; to the spectators, however, the joke is bitterly comic because the torturers are actually exposing their own folly. Once again, the torturers do not see beyond their game to consider that Christ may be involved in a tournament on a much higher level, and their overlooking the possibility that the Christ-knight metaphor may indeed be appropriate further develops the sophisticated irony in the play.

The same spirit of jovial exaggeration continues as the torturers bind Christ to the cross. Unlike the graphic, yet skeletal, treatment in the York cycle, for example, the Towneley version amplifies and repeats the physical details of the Crucifixion. Having already presented their "instruments of torture" to the audience, the torturers compliment one another on their skill as they stretch Christ's body and drive nails through his hands and feet. Even the raising of the cross becomes cause for a lively contest, and each torturer welcomes the opportunity to show his strength:

> Secundus tortor. Sen thou will so haue, here for
> me!
> how draw I, as myght thou the?
> Tercius tortor. Thou drew right wele.
> haue here for me half a foyte!
> quartus tortor. wema, man! I trow thou doyte!
> Thou flyt it neuer a dele;

208

> Bot haue for me here that I may!
> <u>primus tortor</u>. Well drawen, son, bi this day!
> Thou gose well to thi warke!
>
> (179-87)

This morbid enjoyment of Christ's suffering extends even to what must have been the visual climax of the cycles, the elevation of the cross. As the torturers brutally drop the cross into the mortise and once again mock Christ, the playwright contrasts the colossal visual symbol with the clamor of the ignorant men. In such a stirring fusion of commotion and quiet strength, of self-indulgence and self-sacrifice, Christ finally speaks.

The Towneley dramatist expands the biblical source material so that Christ responds to the abuses of the torturers. Instead of addressing the torturers directly, however, Christ speaks to a much larger audience--presumably both the throngs at Calvary and the crowds in the medieval market-place. His speech re-sounds with neither comfort in the Resurrection nor focused condemnation of the torturers, but with pathetic reminders of his wounds and piercing questions about who is responsible for them:

> Behold if euer ye sagh body
> Buffet & bett thus blody,
> Or yit thus dulfully dight;
> In warld was neuer no wight
> That suffred half so sare.
> My mayn, my mode, my myght,
> Is noght bot sorow to sight,
> And comforth none, bot care.
>
> My folk, what haue I done to the,
> That thou all thus shall tormente me?
>
> (236-45)

The spectators' compassion for Christ's suffering is complicated once the piteous list of wounds is interrupted with an accusa-

tion.   In accordance with the medieval tradition which emphasized that Christ's torment continues with each man's sin, the
playwright does not allow detached criticism of the Jews who
crucified Christ.   Instead, each spectator is forced to witness
the biblical Crucifixion as a symbol of both Christ's continuing
sacrifice and mankind's continuing sin.   Thus, spirituality is
not lost, as McNeir mistakenly suggests, but is heightened by
the   dramatist's   "insistence   on   the   physical   agonies   of
Calvary."[20]

The thematic climax toward which the playwright moves
reiterates the contemporaneity of guilt in Christ's suffering.
As he concludes his long, detailed lament from the cross, Christ
offers to God the familiar prayer that the torturers be for-
given:

> Bot, fader, that syttys in trone,
>   fforgyf thou them this gylt,
> I pray to the this boyn,
> Thay wote not what thay doyn,
>   Nor whom thay haue thus spylt.
>
> (290-94)

The spiritual blindness alluded to and demonstrated in the
earlier Passion plays of the Towneley cycle is at last stated
directly and without irony.   A surprising twist to this revelation, however, is the torturers' audacious response to Christ's
prayer.   Instead of coming to their senses--or at least fading
from the scene--the torturers retort about their superior knowledge and their power over Christ:

> <u>primus tortor</u>. yis, what we do full well we knaw.
> <u>ijus tortor</u>. yee, that shall he fynde within a
>   thraw.
>
> (295-96)

In addition to shocking the audience with a painful reminder of the extreme blindness of the torturers, such comments implicitly continue the forceful depiction of medieval sin. The biblical characters had only prophecies and hearsay about miracles to convince them of the divinity of Christ, and although their crime is no less horrible because of their ignorance, it is understandable. The medieval spectators, however, have the capacity to commit an even greater sin, for in spite of their access to biblical history, they continue to injure Christ through failing to follow his teachings.

The subsequent shaking and dropping of the cross in an attempt to break Christ's body--as well as Mary's graphic lament at the sight of her crucified son--reinforce brutally the contemporary responsibility for Christ's pain. What began as a festive sport thus builds to an intense examination of conscience, and the spectators are encouraged to turn their uneasiness inward. The discomfort caused by irreverent yoking of coarse humor and divine mystery is in this play transformed into personal anguish, as the heinous actions of the torturers are meshed with the spectators' own.[21]

The playwright is careful to control this emotion, however, for to leave his audience in a state of self-condemnation and despair would be an unfair and blasphemous misuse of the dramatic medium. Instead, the Towneley dramatist allows his spectators to play with such dark emotions as a means of intensifying the joyful acceptance of the Resurrection. By acknowledging their guilt through involvement in the chaotic scenes presented

on stage, the spectators welcome the "bargain" Christ offers to
them:

> Blo and blody thus am I bett,
> Swongen with swepys & all to-swett,
>   Mankynde, for thi mysdede!
> ffor my luf lust when Wold thou lett,
> And thi harte sadly sett,
>   Sen I thus for the haue blede?
>
> (469-74)

Such an invitation is dramatically and theologically satisfying,
for it promises expedient resolution of the tension which has
long persisted in this cycle, and it reminds the audience of the
spiritual benefits achieved through Christ's sacrifice. The
triumphant presentations of the Harrowing of Hell and the Resurrection become real celebrations for those who have worked
through this emotional process.

The deliberate inclusion of comic elements in the Passion
sequences thus constitutes a significant achievement on the part
of medieval dramatists, who had the insight to recognize that
jubilant acceptance of divine mystery is best accomplished
through emotional involvement. Comic characterization and
development create a confusing blur of earthly and spiritual
priorities, of the Old and New Laws, and of the fear and wonder
possible in miracles; and from this perspective the spectators
acquire a renewed sense of their need for repentance. More
importantly, the plays push the audience to challenge and then
accept emotionally the overwhelming possibility of God's forgiveness and to stand in joy and awe as that possibility is
vividly, dramatically confirmed.

Notes

[1] Waldo F. McNeir, "The Corpus Christi Passion Plays as Dramatic Art," _Studies in Philology_, 48 (1951), 614. McNeir summarizes early twentieth-century attitudes toward the humor in these plays by stating that "it eases momentarily the strain of the Passion, functioning as counterpoint or dramatic relief."

[2] For summaries of this tradition in medieval literature, see Hardin Craig, "The Origin of the Passion Play: Matters of Theory as well as Fact," in _Studies in Honor of A.H.R. Fairchild_, ed. Charles T. Prouty (Columbia: University of Missouri Press, 1946), pp. 81-90; and T.W. Craik, "Violence in the English Miracle Plays," in _Medieval Drama_, ed. Neville Denny (New York: Crane, Russak, & Company, Inc., 1973), pp. 176-77. For a detailed discussion of the Passion and Crucifixion as represented in medieval art, see Gertrud Schiller, _Iconography of Christian Art_, trans. Janet Seligman (1968; rpt. Greenwich, Connecticut: New York Graphic Society Ltd, 1976), II, 88-164.

[3] "Candlemas Day and the Kyllynge of the Children of Israell," in _The Digby Plays_, ed. F.J. Furnivall (1896; rpt. Early English Text Society, e.s. 70, London: Oxford University Press, 1967), 1. 139. Subsequent references to the Digby Massacre play shall be to this edition and cited by line numbers in parentheses.

[4] See Carol Billman, "Grotesque Humor in Medieval Biblical Comedy," _American Benedictine Review_, 31 (1980), 406-17.

[5] See, for example, Nelvin Vos, _For God's Sake Laugh!_ (Richmond, Virginia: John Knox Press, 1967). Vos argues that "laughter reveals . . . the juxtaposition of the derisive scornful laughter of the Inferno with the delightful joy of Paradise," and he explains that "one's relationship to God is the biggest laugh of all," p. 25. See also William F. Lynch, _Christ and Apollo: The Dimensions of the Literary Imagination_ (New York: Sheed and Ward, 1960); and Paul H. Grawe, _Comedy in Space, Time, and the Imagination_ (Chicago: Nelson-Hall, 1983), pp. 287-300.

[6] Clifford Davidson, "The Realism of the York Realist and the York Passion," _Speculum_, 50 (1975), 271.

[7] In Davies, p. 83.

[8] In Davies, p. 111.

[9] In Davies, p. 211. See also lyric 24 in Davies' edition, which consists almost entirely of dialogue between Mary and Christ at the Crucifixion, pp. 86-88.

[10] Davies, p. 38.

[11] For a discussion of possible staging of the Crucifixion, as influenced by pictorial representations, see M.D. Anderson, p. 148.

[12] See especially Gay, pp. 135-40. Gay argues convincingly that the elaborate stage directions of this cycle--particularly those of the Passion plays--provide strong evidence for "place-and-scaffold" staging.

[13] Billman suggests that such chaos--which results from "grotesque black comedy"--constitutes an important feature of both the medieval cycles and modern tragicomedy, such as the works of Beckett, Ionesco, or Pinter. The effect is to portray "a cosmos out of control . . ., a cosmos where man is frustrated in his attempts to communicate, where brutal actions occur without motivation, where people ludicrously act out their roles . . ." p. 416.

[14] McNeir emphasizes that Percula is both "an ornament to her husband's high estate . . . [and] a foil to the Virgin Mary," p. 611.

[15] See J.W. Robinson, "The Art of the York Realist," _Modern Philology_, 60 (1963), 245. Robinson suggests that this emphasis on "mental processes" as well as "processes of behavior" is the distinctive mark of the York Realist.

[16] Kolve, p. 180. Kolve provides a useful analysis of the game substitutions made in the Passion plays, pp. 178-82.

[17] For a detailed explanation of the etymology and connotations of this insult, see Lorrayne Y. Baird, "'Cockes face' and the Problem of poydrace in Chester Passion," _Comparative Drama_, 16 (1982), 227-37. Baird suggests several possibilities for the term _poydrace_ (pewee-ars in the Lumiansky-Mills edition) and provides useful insight into the _Christus gallinaceus_ (Christcock) tradition which the Chester playwright toys with in his nonce-oath.

[18] See Woolf, pp. 254-55. Woolf points out that the childish games played at the Crucifixion in all but the Chester cycle are also characteristic of some Continental scenes.

[19] Woolf, p. 259.

[20] McNeir, p. 622.

[21] See Stephen Spector, "Anti-Semitism and the English Mystery Plays," _Comparative Drama_, 13 (1979), 3-16. Spector extends to the mystery plays Freud's conception of the anti-Semite, "a person who condemns in the Jew those qualities, real or attributed, that he cannot tolerate in his experience or in himself," p. 4. In the drama, Spector explains, the Jews represent "the spirit of disbelief, self-interest, and spiritual

214

blindness" so that "the auditor . . . [may] expel the Jew from himself," p. 13.

CONCLUSION

The "noble gyn" of comedy in the Middle English cycle plays has the capacity for surprising the spectators and providing them with complex, new perspectives on the mysteries of their faith. In their attention to detail, in their well-developed dramatic situations and characters, and in their carefully paced action, the Corpus Christi playwrights establish unlikely parallels between the central mysteries of Christianity--Creation and divine authority, Incarnation, and Crucifixion--and the coarse, often unruly human context in which such mysteries must be understood. Such parallels teach an essential intellectual lesson, for they demonstrate that one may, by glancing around himself instead of heavenward, experience some sense of the divine.

On a dramatic level, the comedy of the plays energizes the traditional biblical narratives and encourages strong involvement from the spectators. In the best plays, the dramatists carefully elicit intense comic response, then transform it into profound spiritual involvement. As a result, the production of the cycle plays--the culmination of focused community effort-- becomes a highly personal means of confronting and resolving religious doubts; and the enjoyment of the humorous plays becomes an important transition to emotional acceptance of divine mystery.

This transition is evident first in the Old Testament plays which focus on Lucifer, Cain and Abel, and Noah. One finds in these plays characters and situations that depart considerably from the biblical tradition and that obviously are intended to be humorous. Cain is coarse and brutal, both in his physical presence--suggested in his dialogues with Abel and, in some cases, his plowboy--and in his rebellious attitude toward his religious duty. It seems clear that the slapstick humor when Cain is present on stage would have evoked genuine, spontaneous laughter in the audience--not only because they were made nervous by his verbal abuse of Abel and even of God, but because the spectators enjoy the comedy itself. If the character of Cain were one-dimensional and allegorical, one would be led to believe that the audience laughs _at_ Cain and the exposure of his follies; yet it is Abel who is developed as a weak, boring character, a development which brings into question the underlying dramatic motivation at work in these plays. Man's stupidity in opposing God's plan--so evident in a character like Cain--is one source of laughter for the audience.

What one encounters in Corpus Christi drama is more than a comedy of situation that provides a laughable inferior from whom members of the audience may learn. And instead of the melodramatic sense of antagonist and protagonist that the audience might expect to find, in which sympathy is given Abel and righteous indignation is directed toward Cain, the plays that use humor most effectively place the members of the audience in the uncomfortable position of knowing what they _should_ do, but doing just the opposite. The spectators, knowing very well that they should in their hearts defend the actions and spirit of the innocent Abel, nevertheless find Cain interesting, amusing, and attractive, instead of horrible. The dramatists are deceptive, for they encourage the members of the audience to share emotionally in Cain's sin by involving them, unawares, in the same struggle. The spectators, like Cain, are thus led to understand their weaknesses and to prepare for the following plays with humility instead of pride.

In the dramatic presentations of Noah and his wife, the playwrights use humor in a similar way to bring the audience to an estimation of its willingness to sacrifice the comforts and rewards of this world and to maintain hope in the next. The characterization of Noah's wife is deliberately molded to evoke the spectators' responses to anti-feminist literature and tradition; her shrewishness, her recalcitrance, and her lack of trust in the plans that Noah and God have for her are clearly intended to cause members of the audience to laugh heartily. Yet the laughter is not directed squarely at Noah's wife, for the plan to escape the flood appears to be only the ludicrous whim of a man who is five hundred years old. The dramatist strives to involve the audience, through comedy, in the struggle between husband and wife and thus imperceptibly involve each viewer in his own struggle between the rational, comprehensible nature of his mind and the often illogical trust upon which his religious beliefs are grounded.

Comedy functions, then, in these Old Testament plays, as a means by which the audience learns about the Old Law and the model of faith that it offers to them. Obedience and rebellion are central themes of these plays, and here playwrights begin to suggest that the principles of order and logic in the world of man do not help him to understand divine mysteries.

More direct confrontation with one of these mysteries, the Incarnation, is at the center of the cycle plays about Joseph and the shepherds. Joseph, like Noah, is characterized primarily as a feeble old man, apparently lacking the wits to understand what God is asking of him. The facts of Mary's pregnancy confound him, and the plays focus on the joke of the cuckolded husband and his young wife. To a typical modern audience, aware of Joseph as a saint, the _fabliau_ which is so clearly a part of the background of the plays seems blasphemous. The medieval audience, too, must have been surprised by this full expansion of a motif that is only faintly suggested in narratives of the time. The vulgar implications of Joseph's yelling to Mary, "Vndo ʒour dore," for example, were certainly not expected by the medieval audience. Yet that audience--more so than a modern one--tolerated the discrepancy between its expectations and the actual scenes on stage, and, in this case, delighted in the humor of the shocking juxtaposition. The audience laughs at Joseph and at his bungling attempts to piece together the details of the unusual story his betrothed has told him, for the audience already knows that, when analyzed logically, the Incarnation does not and cannot make sense. Because Joseph is a well-rounded, appealing, and generally familiar character, however, the members of the audience are brought to examine the divine mystery with the same critical perspective, to acknowledge their own doubts about how--in spite of all rational evidence against it--the Incarnation could possibly occur. The humor of the plays about Joseph therefore involves the audience both playfully and seriously in its own confrontation between sincere, unquestioning faith and rational doubt.

Drama portraying the shepherds on the night of Christ's birth, like the plays of Joseph and his doubts, surprises the audience by shifting the location of most of the action from the Bethlehem stable to the Yorkshire countryside and the tone of the presentation from solemn and reverent to coarse and boisterous. The effect is that the audience becomes intensely involved with the stage action and the characters that bustle about in anything but reverent guises; yet that involvement is always tense, for the audience knows--even if the shepherds do not--what is to happen in the stable and how they are to react to this miraculous event. The playwrights achieve this dramatic effect by introducing comic, contemporary characters that appear nowhere in the biblical source; by interjecting anachronistic elements that interfere with a purely historical understanding of the message of the plays; and by moving the spectators, as well as the shepherds, to be filled with awe as they witness, once again, the Christmas story.

The playwrights thus seek to use humor in these Nativity plays to involve their audiences in a true Advent spirit. Because they laugh at and identify with the characters of these plays, spectators play with the same questions as Joseph and the shepherds about the meaning of Christ's arrival. For them, however, the questions have double significance: they recognize both the historical meaning of the Nativity and the implied contemporaneity of such a monumental event in their faith. Especially on the feast of Corpus Christi, the audience needs to understand that Christ's coming can be an everyday event. Such a realization also prepares the audience to watch the plays of Christ's ministry and Passion with a renewed sense of awe and devotion.

Plays depicting the massacre of the innocents are chronologically akin to the Nativity sequences, but their comic emphasis on the horrible details of the slaughter creates a tension which associates them more closely with the Passion plays. Especially in the characterization of the knights who carry out Herod's order, the playwrights introduce comic developments. These bungling knights arm themselves for battle against infants and play games with the children as the murders are boldly enacted on stage. Several of the cycle dramatists comically expand their source material as they shatter the image of the grieving mothers. The women in these play defy the cowardly knights in horrible, humorous clashes of swords and spindles.

Beneath the surface of this comedy, however, is a profound tension created by the incongruity of tone and subject matter. Despite their audacious attacks on the king's knights, the women are overcome and the children are viciously killed. And although the exaggerated pride of Herod and the trepidation of his knights may amuse the audience, the relentless violence of these plays strains the laughter which may be evoked.

The Passion plays, some of the most vivid of the cycles, sustain such a tension not only in their presentations of the brutality of the Crucifixion, but also in their focus on the horrible games that the torturers play. Most modern audiences would be incredulous at the idea of any comic development in such serious religious drama, and the medieval spectators, one may well imagine, were no less horrified. Unlike the comic response elicited by the Old Testament and Nativity plays, the coupling of these often grotesque representations of Christ's suffering and the menacing games of the mobs encourage profound, intense silence instead of raucous laughter. The silence of Christ throughout his trial and Crucifixion is sharply contrasted with the turmoil about him, and the audience is placed in the uncomfortable position of finding that silence both reassuring and terribly unsettling. It is at once a symbolic suggestion of the distance between Christ and the men who brought about his death, and--in accordance with medieval Christian tradition--a painful, unspoken reminder to the spectators that they, too, are responsible for the Crucifixion. Consequently, the humor in these plays, as in those surrounding the Nativity, serves to add complexity to what appears, on surface level, to be an event of mere historical significance. The underlying theology and purpose of the mystery cycles is revealed in the Passion sequences, and the playwrights strive consciously for an understanding of that theology on an emotional, not rational, level.

One may therefore see that the humorous developments in the

plays are not intrusions, as early criticism assumed, but rather integral and dynamic supports for the vast themes implied in a dramatic presentation of sacred history. The cycle playwrights chose comedy as a "noble gyn" for instruction--both on rational and emotional levels--whereas their contemporaries chose more serious means to communicate the same message. Middle English sermons use serious moralistic tones and numerous, vivid examples to convince listeners of their need for repentance. One may well assume that the sermons and religious tracts in medieval England were successful rhetorically, capable of moving congregations to recall their obligations as Christians. Yet the playwrights who adapted the same religious stories and principles to a dramatic situation chose a very different form of expression, one that sought more than a visual presentation of homiletic message and organization. The playwrights fused doctrine with intense dramatic situation through the use of humor. Because the plays were performed for more than two centuries, it is clear that the cycles were socially and culturally popular, but the main point of this study is that they were also spiritually successful, involving the audience intensely and seriously--often through humorous situation and development.

BIBLIOGRAPHY

Editions of the Cycle Plays

Block, K.S., ed. Ludus Coventriae or the Plaie Called Corpus Christi. Early English Text Society, e.s. 120. 1922; rpt. London: Oxford University Press, 1974.

Davis, Norman and Osborn Waterhouse, eds. Non-Cycle Plays and Fragments. Early English Text Society, s.s. 1. London: Oxford University Press, 1970.

Deimling, Hermann, ed. The Chester Plays, I. Early English Text Society, e.s. 62. 1892; rpt. London: Oxford University Press, 1967.

England, George and Alfred W. Pollard, eds. The Towneley Plays. Early English Text Society, e.s. 71. 1897; rpt. London: Oxford University Press, 1966.

Furnivall, Frederick J., ed. The Digby Plays. 1896; rpt. Early English Tex Society, e.s. 70. London: Oxford University Press, 1967.

Lumiansky, R.M. and David Mills, eds. The Chester Mystery Cycle. Early English Text Society, s.s. 3. London: Oxford University Press, 1974.

Matthews, J., ed. The Chester Plays, II. Early English Text Society, e.s. 115. 1914; rpt. London: Oxford University Press, 1967.

Smith, Lucy Toulmin, ed. York Mystery Plays. 1885; rpt. New York: Russell & Russell, 1968.

Other Primary Sources

Banks, Mary Macleod, ed. An Alphabet of Tales: An English 15th Century Translation of the Alphabetum Narrationum of Etienne de Besancon. Early English Text Society, o.s. 126. London: Oxford University Press, 1904.

Brandeis, Arthur, ed. Jacob's Well: An Englisht Treatise on the Cleansing of Man's Conscience, I. Early English Text Society, o.s. 115. London: Oxford University Press, 1900.

Cowper, J. Meadows, ed. Meditations on the Supper of our Lord, and the Hours of the Passion. 1875, Early English Text Society, o.s. 60; rpt. New York: Kraus Reprint Co., 1975.

Davies, R.T., ed. Medieval English Lyrics: A Critical Anthology. Evanston, Illinois: Northwestern University Press,

1964.

Dyboski, Roman, ed. Songs, Carols, and Other Miscellaneous Poems from the Balliol MS. 354, Richard Hill's Commonplace-Book. Early English Text Society, e.s. 101. London: Oxford University Press, 1907.

Flügel, Ewald, ed. "Liedersammlungen des XVI. Jahrhunderts, besonders aus der Zeit Heinrichs VIII, III." Anglia, 26 (1903), 94-285.

Foster, Frances A., ed. A Stanzaic Life of Christ. Early English Text Society, o.s. 166. London: Oxford University Press, 1924.

Francis, W. Nelson, ed. The Book of Vices and Virtues: A Fourteenth Century English Translation of the Somme le Roi of Lorens D'Orleans. Early English Text Society, o.s. 217. 1942; rpt. London: Oxford University Press, 1968.

Furnivall, Frederick J., ed. Robert of Brunne's "Handlyng Synne." Early English Text Society, o.s. 119, 123; 1901, 1903; rpt. Millwood, New York: Kraus Reprint Co., 1978.

Hulme, William Henry. The Middle-English Harrowing of Hell and Gospel of Nicodemus. 1907; rpt. Early English Text Society, e.s. 100. London: Oxford University Press, 1961.

Lumby, J. Rawson, ed. Ratis Raving, and Other Moral and Religious Pieces, in Prose and Verse. 1870, Early English Text Society, o.s. 43; rpt. New York: Greenwood Press, 1969.

Morris, Richard, ed. Cursor Mundi: A Northumbrian Poem of the XIVth Century. 1874-78; rpt. Early English Text Society, o.s. 57, 59, 62, 66, 68. London: Oxford University Press, 1961.

----------. The Proverbs of Alfred. In An Old English Miscellany. 1872, Early English Text Society, o.s. 49; rpt. New York: Greenwood Press, 1969.

Ross, Woodburn O., ed. Middle English Sermons. 1940; rpt. Early English Text Society, n.s. 209. London: Oxford University Press, 1960.

Simmons, Thomas Frederick, ed. The Lay Folks Mass Book, or The Manner of Hearing Mass. 1879; rpt. Early English Text Society, o.s. 71. London: Oxford University Press, 1968.

Secondary Sources

Adams, Joseph Quincy. Chief Pre-Shakespearean Dramas: A Selection of Plays Illustrating the History of the English Drama

from its Origin down to Shakespeare. Boston: Houghton
Mifflin Company, 1924.

Adolf, Helen. "On Mediaeval Laughter." Speculum, 22 (1947),
251-53.

Allen, Don Cameron. The Legend of Noah. Illinois Studies in
Language and Literature, 33. Urbana: University of Illinois Press, 1949.

Anderson, M.D. Drama and Imagery in English Medieval Churches.
1955; rpt. Cambridge: Cambridge University Press, 1963.

Anderson, Michael. "The Comedy of Greece and Rome." In Comic
Drama: The European Heritage. Ed. W.D. Howarth. 1978;
rpt. New York: St. Martin's Press, 1979, pp. 22-39.

Baird, Joseph L. and Lorrayne Y. Baird. "Fabliau Form and the
Hegge Joseph's Return." The Chaucer Review, 8 (1973),
159-69.

Baird, Lorrayne Y. "'Cockes face' and the Problem of poydrace
in the Chester Passion." Comparative Drama, 16 (1982),
227-37.

Bates, Katharine Lee. The English Religious Drama. 1893; rpt.
New York: The Macmillan Company, 1909.

Baugh, Albert Croll. "The Beginnings of the Drama." In A
Literary History of England. New York: Appleton-Century-
Crofts, Inc., 1948, I, pp. 273-87.

Bentley, Eric. "Farce." In Comedy: Meaning and Form. Ed.
Robert W. Corrigan. San Francisco: Chandler Publishing
Company, 1965, pp. 279-303.

Bergson, Henri. "Laughter." 1900; rpt. in Comedy. Ed. Wylie
Sypher. Baltimore: The Johns Hopkins University Press,
1980.

Bevington, David M. From Mankind to Marlowe: Growth of Structure in the Popular Drama of Tudor England. Cambridge,
Massachusetts: Harvard University Press, 1962.

Billman, Carol. "Grotesque Humor in Medieval Biblical Comedy."
American Benedictine Review, 31 (1980), 406-17.

Boone, Blair W. "The Skill of Cain in the English Mystery
Cycles." Comparative Drama, 16 (1982), 112-29.

Brewer, Derek. "Notes toward a Theory of Medieval Comedy." In
Medieval Comic Tales. Trans. Peter Rickard, Alan Deyer-
mond, Derek Brewer, David Blamiris, Peter King, and Michael
Lapridge. Totowa, New Jersey: Rowman and Littlefield,

1973, pp. 140-60.

Brockman, Bennett A. "The Law of Man and the Peace of God: Judicial Process as Satiric Theme in the Wakefield Mactatio Abel." Speculum, 49 (1974), 699-707.

Browne, E. Martin. "Producing the Mystery Plays for Modern Audiences." Drama Survey, 3 (1963), 5-15.

Cady, Frank W. "The Passion Group in Towneley." Modern Philology, 10 (1913), 587-600.

Campbell, Josie P. "Farce as Function in the Wakefield Shepherds' Plays." Chaucer Review, 14 (1980), 336-43.

Caputi, Anthony. Buffo: The Genius of Vulgar Comedy. Detroit: Wayne State University Press, 1978.

Carey, Millicent. The Wakefield Group in the Towneley Cycle: A Study to Determine the Conventional and Original Elements in Four Plays Commonly Ascribed to the Wakefield Author. Baltimore: The Johns Hopkins Press, 1930.

Cawley, A.C. "The 'Grotesque' Feast in the Prima Pastorum." Speculum, 30 (1955), 213-17.

----------. "Iak Garcio of the Prima Pastorum." Modern Language Notes, 68 (1953), 169-72.

Cazamian, Louis. The Development of English Humour, I: From the Early Times to the Renascence. New York: The Macmillan Company, 1930.

Chambers, E.K. The Mediaeval Stage. 2 vols. London: Oxford University Press, 1903.

Chidamian, Claude. "Mak and the Tossing in the Blanket." Speculum, 22 (1947), 186-90.

Coffman, George R. "The Miracle Play in England--Nomenclature." PMLA, 31 (1916), 448-65.

----------. "A Plea for the Study of the Corpus Christi Plays as Drama." Studies in Philology, 26 (1929), 411-24.

Coletti, Theresa. "Devotional Iconography in the N-Town Marian Plays." Comparative Drama, 11 (1977), 22-44.

Collins, Patrick J. "Narrative Bible Cycles in Medieval Art and Drama." Comparative Drama, 9 (1975), 125-46.

----------. "Typology, Criticism, and Medieval Drama: Some Observations on Method." Comparative Drama, 10 (1976-77), 298-313.

Cook, Albert. _The Dark Voyage and the Golden Mean: A Philosophy of Comedy_. Cambridge, Massachusetts: Harvard University Press, 1949.

Corrigan, Robert W. "Comedy and the Comic Spirit." In _Comedy: Meaning and Form_. Ed. Robert W. Corrigan. San Francisco: Chandler Publishing Company, 1965, pp. 1-11.

Cosbey, Robert C. "The Mak Story and Its Folklore Analogues." _Speculum_, 20 (1945), 310-17.

Craig, Hardin. _English Religious Drama of the Middle Ages_. 1955; rpt. London: Oxford University Press, 1967.

----------. "The Origin of the Passion Play: Matters of Theory as well as Fact." In _Studies in Honor of A.H.R. Fairchild_. Ed. Charles T. Prouty. Columbia: University of Missouri Press, 1946, pp. 81-90.

Craik, T.W. "Violence in the English Miracle Plays." In _Medieval Drama_. Ed. Neville Denny. New York: Crane, Russak, & Company, Inc., 1973, pp. 173-95.

Cutts, John P. "The Shepherds' Gifts in _The Second Shepherds' Play_ and Bosch's 'Adoration of the Magi'." _Comparative Drama_, 4 (1970), 120-24.

Davenport, W.A. _Fifteenth-century English Drama: The Early Moral Plays and their Literary Relations_. Cambridge: D.S. Brewer, 1982.

Davidson, Clifford. "After the Fall: Design in the Old Testament Plays in the York Cycle." _Mediaevalia_, 1 (1975), 1-24.

----------. "The Realism of the York Realist and the York Passion." _Speculum_, 50 (1975), 270-83.

Dean, James. "The World Grown Old and Genesis in Middle English Historical Writings." _Speculum_, 57 (1982), 548-68.

Deasy, Philip Cormac. _St. Joseph in the English Mystery Plays_. Washington, D.C.: Catholic University Press, 1937.

Diller, Hans-Jürgen. "The Craftsmanship of the Wakefield Master." 1965; rpt. in _Medieval English Drama: Essays Critical and Contextual_. Ed. Jerome Taylor and Alan H. Nelson. Chicago: The University of Chicago Press, 1972, pp. 245-59.

Dorrell, Margaret. "Two Studies of the York Corpus Christi Play." _Leeds Studies in English_, N.S. 6 (1972), 63-111.

Duncan, Robert L. "Comedy in the English Mysteries: Three

Versions of the Noah Story." *Illinois Quarterly*, 35 (1973), 5-14.

Dunn, E. Catherine. "Lyrical Form and the Prophetic Principle in the Towneley Plays." *Medieval Studies*, 23 (1961), 80-90.

----------. "Popular Devotion in the Vernacular Drama of Medieval England." *Medievalia et Humanistica*, 4 (1973), 55-68.

Duprey, Richard. "Whatever Happened to Comedy?" 1962; rpt. in *Comedy: Meaning and Form*. Ed. Robert W. Corrigan. San Francisco: Chandler Publishing Company, 1965, pp. 243-49.

Dutka, JoAnna. "Mysteries, Minstrels, and Music." *Comparative Drama*, 8 (1974), 112-24.

Earl, James W. "The Shape of Old Testament History in the Towneley Plays." *Studies in Philology*, 69 (1972), 434-52.

Elliott, John R., Jr. "A Checklist of Modern Production of the Medieval Mystery Cycles in England." *Research Opportunities in Renaissance Drama*, 13-14 (1970-71), 259-66.

Emerson, Oliver F. "Legends of Cain, Especially in Old and Middle English." *PMLA*, 21 (1906), 831-929.

Feibleman, James. *In Praise of Comedy: A Study of its Theory and Practice*. New York: Russell & Russell, 1962.

Fifield, Merle. "Quod quaeritis, o discipuli." *Comparative Drama*, 5 (1971), 53-69.

Foster, Frances A. "The Mystery Plays and the *Northern Passion*." *Modern Language Notes*, 26 (1911) 169-71.

Fry, Christopher. "Comedy." 1951; rpt. in *Comedy: Meaning and Form*. Ed. Robert W. Corrigan. San Francisco: Chandler Publishing Company, 1965, pp. 15-17.

Fry, Timothy, O.S.B. "The Antiquity of the Tradition of the Triads in the English Cycle Plays." *American Benedictine Review*, 18 (1967), 465-81.

----------. "The Unity of the *Ludus Coventriae*." *Studies in Philology*, 48 (1951), 527-70.

Gardiner, Harold C., S.J. *Mysteries' End: An Investigation of the Last Days of the Medieval Religious Stage*. 1946; rpt. New York: Archon Books, 1967.

Gardner, John. "Imagery and Allusion in the Wakefield Noah Play." *Papers on Language and Literature*, 4 (1968), 3-12.

----------. The Construction of the Wakefield Cycle. Carbondale: Southern Illinois University Press, 1974.

Gauvin, Claude. "Rite et jeu dans le theatre religieux anglais du Moyen Age." Revue d'Histoire du Theatre, 29 (1977), 128-40.

Gay, Anne Cooper. "The 'Stage' and the Staging of the N-Town Plays." Research Opportunities in Renaissance Drama, 10 (1967), 135-40.

Gayley, Charles Mills. Plays of Our Forefathers and Some of the Traditions upon Which They Were Founded. 1907; rpt. New York: Biblo and Tannen, 1968.

Gibson, Gail McMurray. "'Porta haec clausa erit': Comedy, Conception, and Ezekiel's Closed Door in the Ludus Coventriae Play of 'Joseph's Return'." Journal of Medieval and Renaissance Studies, 8 (1978), 137-56.

----------. "Bury St. Edmunds, Lydgate, and the N-Town Cycle." Speculum, 56 (1981), 56-90.

Grawe, Paul H. Comedy in Space, Time and the Imagination. Chicago: Nelson-Hall, 1983.

Greg, W.W. Bibliographical and Textual Problems of the English Miracle Cycles. London: Alexander Moring Limited, 1914.

Grove, Thomas N. "Light in Darkness: The Comedy of the York 'Harrowing of Hell' as Seen against the Backdrop of the Chester 'Harrowing of Hell'." Neuphilologische Mitteilungen, 75 (1974), 115-25.

Haden, Roger Lee. "'Ilike a Creature, Takes Entente': A Re-Investigation of the Purpose and Effectiveness of Medieval Corpus Christi Drama." Emporia State Research Studies, 27 (1978), 5-33.

Hanks, Dorrel T., Jr. "The Mactacio Abel and the Wakefield Cycle: A Study in Context." Southern Quarterly, 16 (1977), 47-57.

Hanning, R.W. "'You Have Begun a Parlous Pleye': The Nature and Limits of Dramatic Mimesis as a Theme in Four Middle English 'Fall of Lucifer' Cycle Plays." Comparative Drama, 7 (1973), 22-50.

Hardison, O.B., Jr. Christian Rite and Christian Drama. Baltimore: The Johns Hopkins University Press, 1965.

Hare, Arnold. "English Comedy." In Comic Drama: The European Heritage. Ed. W.D. Howarth. 1978; rpt. New York: St. Martin's Press, 1979, pp. 122-43.

Hartnett, Edith. "Cain in the Medieval Towneley Play." Annuale Mediaevale, 12 (1971), 21-29.

Harty, Kevin J. "The Norwich Grocers Play and Its Three Cyclic Counterparts: Four English Mystery Plays on the Fall of Man." Studia Neophilologica, 53 (1981), 77-89.

----------. "'Unbeleeffee is a Fowle Sinne': The Chester Nativity Play." Susquehanna University Studies, 11 (1979), 35-41.

Harvey, Nancy Lenz and Julia C. Dietrich. "Recent Studies in the Corpus Christi Mystery Plays." English Literary Renaissance, 5 (1975), 396-415.

Heilman, Robert Bechtold. The Ways of the World: Comedy and Society. Seattle: University of Washington Press, 1978.

Hemingway, Samuel B. English Nativity Plays. 1901; rpt. New York: Russell & Russell, 1964.

Hentsch, Alice A. De la Litterature Didactique du Moyen Age, s'adressant specialement aux femmes. Cambridge: Cahors, 1903.

Holding, Peter. "Stagecraft in the York Cycle." Theatre Notebook, 34 (1980), 51-60.

Holland, Norman N. Laughing: A Psychology of Humor. Ithaca, New York: Cornell University Press, 1982.

Howarth, W.D. "Theoretical Considerations." In Comic Drama: The European Heritage. Ed. W.D. Howarth. 1978; rpt. New York: St. Martin's Press, 1979, pp. 1-21.

Hughes, Robert. Heaven and Hell in Western Art. New York: Stein and Day Publishers, 1968.

Huizinga, Johan. Homo-Ludens: A Study of the Play Element in Culture. 1944; rpt. New York: Roy Publishers, 1950.

----------. The Waning of the Middle Ages. 1924; rpt. London: Edward Arnold Ltd., 1970.

Jeffrey, David Lyle. "Stewardship in the Wakefield Mactacio Abel and Noe Plays." American Benedictine Review, 22 (1971), 64-76.

Kahrl, Stanley J. Traditions of Medieval English Drama. 1974; rpt. Pittsburgh: University of Pittsburgh Press, 1975.

Kaul, A.N. The Action of English Comedy: Studies in the Encounter of Abstraction and Experience from Shakespeare to Shaw.

New Haven: Yale University Press, 1970.

Kinghorn, A.M. _Mediaeval Drama_. London: Evans Brothers Limited, 1968.

Knights, L.C. "Notes on Comedy." In _Comedy: Meaning and Form_. Ed. Robert W. Corrigan. San Francisco: Chandler Publishing Company, 1965, pp. 181-91.

Kolve, V.A. _The Play Called Corpus Christi_. Stanford, California: Stanford University Press, 1966.

Langer, Susanne. "The Comic Rhythm." In _Comedy: Meaning and Form_. Ed. Robert W. Corrigan. San Francisco: Chandler Publishing Company, 1965, pp. 119-40.

Leiter, Louis. "Typology, Paradigm, Metaphor, and Image in the York _Creation of Adam and Eve_." _Drama Survey_, 7 (1969), 113-32.

Levin, Harry. "From Play to Plays: The Folklore of Comedy." _Comparative Drama_, 16 (1982), 130-47.

Lumiansky, R.M. "Comedy and Theme in the Chester _Harrowing of Hell_." _Tulane Studies in English_, 10 (1960), 5-12.

Lynch, William F., S.J. _Christ and Apollo: The Dimensions of the Literary Imagination_. New York: Sheed and Ward, 1960.

Mack, Maynard, Jr. "The _Second Shepherds' Play_: A Reconsideration." _PMLA_, 93 (1978), 78-85.

Manly, Joseph Matthews. _Specimens of the Pre-Shakespearean Drama_. 1897; rpt. New York: Biblo and Tannen, 1967.

Manly, William M. "Shepherds and Prophets: Religious Unity in the Towneley _Secunda Pastorum_." _PMLA_, 78 (1963), 151-55.

Marshall, John. "The Medieval English Stage: A Graffito of a Hell-Mouth Scaffold?" _Theatre Notebook_, 34 (1980), 99-103.

Marshall, Linda E. "'Sacral Parody' in the _Secunda Pastorum_." _Speculum_, 47 (1972), 720-36.

Marshall, Mary H. "Aesthetic Values of the Liturgical Drama." 1951; rpt. in _Medieval English Drama: Essays Critical and Contextual_. Ed. Jerome Taylor and Alan H. Nelson. Chicago: The University of Chicago Press, 1972, pp. 28-43.

Matthews, Honor. _The Primal Curse: The Myth of Cain and Abel in the Theatre_. New York: Schocken Books, 1967.

McAlindon, T. "Comedy and Terror in Middle English Literature: The Diabolical Game." _Modern Language Review_, 60 (1965),

323-32.

McClure, Donald S. "Commercialism in the York Mystery Cycle." _Studies in the Humanities_, 2 (1970-71), 32-34.

McCollom, William G. _The Divine Average: A View of Comedy_. Cleveland: The Press of Case Western Reserve University, 1971.

----------. "From Dissonance to Harmony: The Evolution of Early English Comedy." _The Theatre Annual_, 21 (1964), 69-96.

McNeir, Waldo F. "The Corpus Christi Passion Plays as Dramatic Art." _Studies in Philology_, 48 (1951), 601-28.

Meredith, George. "An Essay on Comedy." 1877; rpt. in _Comedy_. Ed. Wylie Sypher. Baltimore: The Johns Hopkins University Press, 1980.

Meyers, Walter. _A Figure Given: Typology in the Wakefield Plays_. Pittsburgh: Duquesne University Press, 1970.

Mill, Anna J. "Medieval Stage Decoration: That Apple Tree Again." _Theatre Notebook_, 24 (1970), 122-24.

----------. "Noah's Wife Again." _PMLA_, 56 (1941), 613-26.

Morgan, Margery M. "'High Fraud': Paradox and Double-Plot in the English Shepherds' Plays." _Speculum_, 39 (1964), 676-89.

Munson, William F. "Audience and Meaning in Two Medieval Dramatic Realisms." _Comparative Drama_, 9 (1975), 44-67.

Nelson, Alan H. "Principles of Processional Staging: York Cycle." In _The Medieval English Stage: Corpus Christi Pageants and Plays_. Chicago: The University of Chicago Press, 1974, pp. 15-37.

----------. "'Sacred' and 'Secular' Currents in _The Towneley Play of Noah_." _Drama Survey_, 3 (1964), 393-401.

----------. "Some Configurations of Staging in Medieval English Drama." In _Medieval English Drama: Essays Critical and Contextual_. Ed. Jerome Taylor and Alan H. Nelson. Chicago: The University of Chicago Press, 1972, pp. 116-47.

Nicoll, Allardyce. "The Religious Drama of the Middle Ages." In _Masks, Mimes and Miracles: Studies in the Popular Theatre_. New York: Cooper Square Publishers, Inc., 1963, pp. 175-213.

Nitecki, Alicia K. "The Sacred Elements of the Secular Feast in _Prima Pastorum_." _Mediaevalia_, 3 (1977), 229-37.

O'Connell, Rosalie M. "Sovereignty through Speech in the Corpus Christi Mystery Plays." *Renascence*, 33 (1981), 117-28.

O'Faolain, Julia and Lauro Martines, eds. *Not in God's Image: Women in History from the Greeks to the Victorians*. London: Maurice Temple Smith Ltd., 1973.

Olson, Elder. *The Theory of Comedy*. Bloomington: Indiana University Press, 1968.

Owst, G.R. *Literature and Pulpit in Medieval England: A Neglected Chapter in the History of English Letters and of the English People*. 1933; rpt. New York: Barnes & Noble, Inc., 1961.

Potter, Stephen. *Sense of Humour*. New York: Henry Holt & Company, 1954.

Prosser, Eleanor. *Drama and Religion in the English Mystery Plays: A Re-Evaluation*. 1961; rpt. Stanford, California: Stanford University Press, 1966.

Remly, Lynn. "*Deus Caritas*: The Christian Message of the 'Secunda Pastorum'." *Neuphilologische Mitteilungen*, 72 (1971), 742-48.

Robertson, D.W., Jr. "The Question of 'Typology' and the Wakefield *Mactacio Abel*." *American Benedictine Review*, 25 (1974), 57-73.

Robinson, J.W. "The Art of the York Realist." *Modern Philology*, 60 (1963), 241-51.

----------. "The Late Medieval Cult of Jesus and the Mystery Plays." *PMLA*, 80 (1965), 508-14.

Roddy, Kevin. "Epic Qualities in the Cycle Plays." In *Medieval Drama*. Ed. Neville Denny. New York: Crane, Russak & Company, Inc., 1973, pp. 155-72.

Ross, Lawrence J. "Symbol and Structure in the *Secunda Pastorum*." 1967; rpt. in *Medieval English Drama: Essays Critical and Contextual*. Ed. Jerome Taylor and Alan H. Nelson. Chicago: University of Chicago Press, 1972, pp. 177-211.

Roston, Murray. *Biblical Drama in England From the Middle Ages to the Present Day*. London: Faber and Faber, 1968.

Ruggiers, Paul G. "Some Theoretical Considerations of Comedy in the Middle Ages." In *Versions of Medieval Comedy*. Ed. Paul G. Ruggiers. Norman: University of Oklahoma Press, 1977.

Salter, F.M. *Mediaeval Drama in Chester*. Toronto: University of Toronto Press, 1955.

Savage, Donald James. "An Analysis of the Comic Element in the Chester, York, Coventry, and Towneley Mystery Cycles." Diss. University of Minnesota, 1955.

Schapiro, Meyer. "'Muscipula Diaboli': The Symbolism of the Merode Altarpiece." *Art Bulletin*, 27 (1945), 182-87.

Schiller, Gertrud. *Iconography of Christian Art*. 2 vols. Trans. Janet Seligman. 1968; rpt. Greenwich, Connecticut: New York Graphic Society Ltd, 1976.

Schilling, Bernard N. *The Comic Spirit: Boccaccio to Thomas Mann*. Detroit: Wayne State University Press, 1965.

Schless, Howard H. "The Comic Element in the Wakefield Noah." In *Studies in Medieval Literature, in Honor of Professor Albert Croll Baugh*. Ed. MacEdward Leach. Philadelphia: University of Pennsylvania Press, 1961, pp. 229-43.

Scott, Nathan A., Jr. "The Bias of Comedy and the Narrow Escape into Faith." 1961; rpt. in *Comedy: Meaning and Form*. Ed. Robert W. Corrigan. San Francisco: Chandler Publishing Company, 1965, pp. 81-115.

Sinanoglou, Leah. "The Christ Child as Sacrifice: A Medieval Tradition and the Corpus Christi Plays." *Speculum*, 48 (1973), 491-509.

Slights, William W.E. "The Incarnations of Comedy." *University of Toronto Quarterly*, 51 (1981), 13-27.

Somerset, J.A.B. "'Fair is foul and foul is fair': Vice-Comedy's Development and Theatrical Effects." In *The Elizabethan Theatre*, V. Ed. G.R. Hibbard. Hamden, Connecticut: The Shoe String Press, Inc., 1975. pp. 54-75.

Spector, Stephen. "Anti-Semitism and the English Mystery Plays." *Comparative Drama*, 13 (1979), 3-16.

Speyser, Suzanne. "Dramatic Illusion and Sacred Reality in the Towneley *Prima Pastorum*." *Studies in Philology*, 78 (1981), 1-19.

Steele, Robert. *Mediaeval Lore from Bartholomew Angelicus*. London: Chatto & Windus, 1924.

Stephenson, Robert C. "Farce as Method." 1961; rpt. in *Comedy: Meaning and Form*. Ed. Robert W. Corrigan. San Francisco: Chandler Publishing Company, 1965.

Stevens, Martin. "The Dramatic Setting of the Wakefield Annunciation." *PMLA*, 81 (1966), 193-98.

----------. *Four Middle English Mystery Cycles*. Princeton, New Jersey: Princeton University Press, 1987.

----------. "Illusion and Reality in the Medieval Drama." *College English*, 32 (1971), 448-64.

----------. "Language as Theme in the Wakefield Plays." *Speculum*, 52 (1977), 100-17.

----------. "The Staging of the Wakefield Plays." *Research Opportunities in Renaissance Drama*, 11 (1968), 115-28.

----------. "The Theatre of the World: A Study in Medieval Dramatic Form." *Chaucer Review*, 7 (1973), 234-49.

Sticca, Sandro. "Drama and Spirituality in the Middle Ages." *Medievalia et Humanistica*, n.s. 4 (1973), 69-87.

Stock, Lorraine Kochanske. "Comedy in the English Mystery Cycles: Three Comic Scenes in the Chester *Shepherds' Play*." In *Versions of Medieval Comedy*. Ed. Paul G. Ruggiers. Norman: University of Oklahoma Press, 1977, pp. 211-26.

Stuart, Donald Clive. "The Stage Setting of Hell and the Iconography of the Middle Ages." *The Romanic Review*, 14 (1913), 330-42.

Taft, Edmund M. "Surprised by Love: The Dramatic Structure and Popular Appeal of the *Wakefield Second Shepherds' Pageant*." *Journal of Popular Culture*, 14 (1980), 131-40.

Tatlock, J.S.P. "Medieval Laughter." *Speculum*, 21 (1947), 287-94.

Taylor, George C. "The Relation of the English Corpus Christi Play to the Middle English Religious Lyric." *Modern Philology*, 5 (1907), 1-38.

Taylor, Henry Osborn. *The Mediaeval Mind: A History of the Development of Thought and Emotion in the Middle Ages*, I. Cambridge, Massachusetts: Harvard University Press, 1966.

Taylor, Jerome. "The Dramatic Structure of the Middle English Corpus Christi, or Cycle, Plays." 1964; rpt. in *Medieval English Drama: Essays Critical and Contextual*. Ed. Jerome Taylor and Alan H. Nelson. Chicago: The University of Chicago Press, 1972, pp. 148-56.

Thompson, Francis J. "Unity in *The Second Shepherds' Tale*." *Modern Language Notes*, 64 (1949), 302-06.

Travis, Peter W. *Dramatic Design in the Chester Cycle*. Chicago: The University of Chicago Press, 1982.

Tydeman, William. "Street Theatre." In *The Theatre in the Middle Ages*. London: Cambridge University Press, 1978, pp. 86-120.

Tyson, Cynthia Haldenby. "Noah's Flood, the River Jordan, the Red Sea: Staging in the Towneley Cycle." *Comparative Drama*, 8 (1974), 101-11.

Vinter, Donna Smith. "Didactic Characterization: the Towneley Abraham." *Comparative Drama*, 14 (1980), 117-36.

Vos, Nelvin. *For God's Sake Laugh!* Richmond, Virginia: John Knox Press, 1967.

Watt, Homer A. "The Dramatic Unity of the 'Secunda Pastorum'." In *Essays and Studies in Honor of Carleton Brown*. New York: New York University Press, 1940, pp. 158-66.

Watts, Harold H. "The Sense of Regain: A Theory of Comedy." 1946; rpt. in *Comedy: Meaning and Form*. Ed. Robert W. Corrigan. San Francisco: Chandler Publishing Company, 1965.

White, Beatrice. "Medieval Mirth." *Anglia*, 78 (1960), 284-301.

Wickham, Glynne. *Early English Stages, I: 1300-1576*. London: Routledge and Kegan Paul, 1966.

----------. "Medieval Comic Traditions and the Beginnings of English Comedy." In *Comic Drama: The European Heritage*. Ed. W.D. Howarth. New York: St. Martin's Press, 1979, pp. 40-62.

Williams, Arnold. "The Comic in the Cycles." In *Medieval Drama*. Ed. Neville Denny. London: Edward Arnold, 1973, pp. 109-23.

----------. *The Drama of Medieval England*. 1961; rpt. Lansing: Michigan State University Press, 1963.

Wimsatt, W.K., Jr. "The Criticism of Comedy." In *English Stage Comedy*. Ed. W.K. Wimsatt, Jr. English Institute Essays, 1954. New York: Columbia University Press, 1955, pp. 3-21.

Withington, Robert. "The Corpus Christi Plays as Drama." *Studies in Philology*, 27 (1930), 573-82.

Wood, Frederik T. "The Comic Elements in the English Mystery Plays." *Neophilologus*, 25 (1940), 39-48, 194-206.

Woolf, Rosemary. _The English Mystery Plays_. 1972; rpt. Berkeley: University of California Press, 1973.

Young, M. James. "The Unity of the English Mystery Cycles." _The Quarterly Journal of Speech_, 58 (1972), 327-37.

Zimbardo, Rose A. "Comic Mockery of the Sacred: _The Frogs_ and _The Second Shepherds' Play_." _Educational Theatre Journal_, 30 (1978), 398-406.

INDEX

Antichrist legend, 9, 152
Antifeminist tradition, 75, 78-81, 82, 87
Cain, 40-66: traditional characterization, 42, 56; as plowman,
     43-44; in Mactacio Abel, 41-66; allegorical significance,
     45
Chaucer, 44, 66
Chester cycle: Adoration, 141-142, 146, 149, 156, 159, 160-62;
     Cain, 60, 61-62; Creation, 32, 39; Drapers' play, 41;
     Massacre of Innocents, 175-177, 182; Nativity, 109, 110,
     129, 137-139; Noah, 70, 71, 72, 73, 81-86, 89-90; Passion
     plays, 185-188, 200-201
Christ, 181, 182, 183, 185-187, 188, 191-211
Creation, 32-40
Crucifixion, 149, 183; see also Passion plays
Cursor Mundi, 68
De Nativitate, 108
Devil: in Cain and Abel plays, 42; in Newcastle Noah play,
     76-78; tradition in N-Town play of trial of Joseph and
     Mary, 133
Digby Massacre of Innocents, 173, 172-175, 177-178, 179-180
Divine Incarnation, 107-108, 114, 122, 125-126, 130, 140, 141,
     149, 162-163
Emotionalism, 183-185
Evolution of drama, 1-5
Exeter Book, 109
Fabliau tradition, 111, 112, 115, 117-118, 119, 123, 124, 126-
     129, 137
First Shepherds' Play, see Prima Pastorum
Garcio, see Pike-harnes
Gnostic Book of Noria, 76
God: Old Testament view, 31; in Creation plays, 32-35; in Mac-
     tacio Abel, 58-59; in Newcastle Noah play, 69; in Chester
     Noah play, 83-84; in Processus Noe, 87
Herod: in Massacre plays, 179-182; in Passion plays, 185, 187,
     190-193
Joseph, 108-130
Judas, 185, 196
Liturgical drama, 3-4, 5, 13
Lucifer, 31-32, 35-40
Mactacio Abel, 41-66
Massacre of the Innocents, 172-183
Medieval law: in Mactacio Abel, 63-64; in N-Town Trial of Joseph
     and Mary, 132-133
Mirrour of the Blessed Lyf of Jesu Christ, 121
New law, 182-183
Newcastle play of Noah, 68-69, 70, 72, 74-75, 76-78
Noah, 31, 66-96
Noah's wife, 75-83, 84, 88-96
N-Town: Betrothal of Mary, 116, 118, 120; Birth of Christ, 137,
     140; Cain and Abel, 45, 54, 60-61, 62; Creation, 33, 34,
     41; Joseph's Return, 113-130; Massacre of Innocents, 176,

178-179; Noah, 70, 72, 73, 84, 95-96; Passion plays, 188-190, 198-200; Salutation and Conception, 115-116; Trial of Joseph and Mary, 131-137; Woman Taken in Adultery, 19-25
Octavian, 137-139
Passion plays, 171-172, 183-211
Percula, 188-190
Pike-harnes, 41, 44-45
Pilate, 185-186, 188-190, 194-195
Prima Pastorum, 10, 141, 142-145, 147, 156-158, 162
Processus Noe, 70-71, 73, 86-96
Protevangelium, 108
Proverbs of Alfred, 79
Pseudo-Matthew, 108
Rules of Marriage, 104
Salome-Tebell (Zelome), 139-141
Satan, see Devil
Second Shepherds' Play, see Secunda Pastorum
Secunda Pastorum, 5-16, 17, 141, 145-146, 147-149, 150-156, 159-160
Shearmen and Taylors' pageant, 109
Shepherds' plays, 108, 130-162
Staging: of Noah plays, 66-67; use of animals, 67; use of central platea, 185; use of hell-mouth, 31; use of water, 93
Tertullian, 79
Towneley: Annunciation, 115, 125; Creation, 33, 34, 41; Joseph, 110-113, 129; Massacre of Innocents, 173-174, 177, 181; Passion plays, 188, 194-198, 201-205, 206-211; see also Mactacio Abel, Prima Pastorum, Processus Noe, Secunda Pastorum
Wakefield plays, see Towneley
York: Cain and Abel, 45; Creation, 32, 34, 41; Joseph, 109-111, 112; Massacre of Innocents, 173, 176; Nativity, 131; Noah, 69, 73, 74, 84, 90; Passion plays, 188-190, 191-194; Temptation and Fall, 39